Italian for Beginners

A Comprehensive Guide for Learning the Italian Language Fast

© **Copyright 2020**

All Rights Reserved. No part of this book may be reproduced in any form without permission in writing from the author. Reviewers may quote brief passages in reviews.

Disclaimer: No part of this publication may be reproduced or transmitted in any form or by any means, mechanical or electronic, including photocopying or recording, or by any information storage and retrieval system, or transmitted by email without permission in writing from the publisher.

While all attempts have been made to verify the information provided in this publication, neither the author nor the publisher assumes any responsibility for errors, omissions or contrary interpretations of the subject matter herein.

This book is for entertainment purposes only. The views expressed are those of the author alone, and should not be taken as expert instruction or commands. The reader is responsible for his or her own actions.

Adherence to all applicable laws and regulations, including international, federal, state and local laws governing professional licensing, business practices, advertising and all other aspects of doing business in the US, Canada, UK or any other jurisdiction is the sole responsibility of the purchaser or reader.

Neither the author nor the publisher assumes any responsibility or liability whatsoever on the behalf of the purchaser or reader of these materials. Any perceived slight of any individual or organization is purely unintentional.

Contents

INTRODUCTION 1
SECTION 1 - BASIS OF GRAMMAR 4
SECTION 2 - VERBAL SYSTEM 32
SECTION 3 - GRAMMAR EXERCISES 59
SECTION 4 - DIALOGUES 76
SECTION 5 - VOCABULARY 115
CONCLUSION 140

Introduction

When a person decides to learn a new language, the reasons can vary—such as for business, tourism, and also "matters of love!" Thus, some of the advantages of learning a language deal with better work opportunities, traveling independently, reading a book or watching a movie in the original language, broadening personal relationships, etc. However, there isn't always a specific need. Sometimes people learn languages only to see the world from another point of view, or to train and stimulate the brain, improving creativity and problem-solving skills. For others, it could represent a hobby, similar to collecting things or playing a sport.

Languages are the reflection of a culture and country. Considering this, one can understand why many people want to learn Italian, even if it is a language that is spoken only in Italy. Its traditions and culture are what make Italian so fascinating. Its literature, art, music, food, and cities are all collected and reflected in the language and how it is expressed and used. Learning Italian means to get into the culture of the country, a place which is the result of the passage of many peoples, languages, and traditions. History has taught us that the culture which most influenced Italy, and so the Italian language, is the Roman one, whose roots are Latin. We also know that Romans spread their culture, language, and legal system almost everywhere. Due to this, there are many similarities between English and Italian, even if their linguistic family and origin are not the same. There are many Latin phrases used every day in English, such as "e.g", which stands for "exempli gratia", "for example", "etc."—which stands for "et cetera" and means "and so on". Or "i.e", which stands for "id est" that means "that is". This are Latin words but ones that are still used in English.

The process of learning a language is not easy and requires both a method and dedication. The purpose of this book is to show you that you can learn a language, no matter how hard it might seem in the beginning.

The first two parts of the book give you all the necessary tools to understand how to create a sentence and orient yourself in the depth of exceptions which characterized Italian as a Latin language.

In the third part, you will find dialogues with a step-by-step translation and some questions with answer keys. This section provides you with a practical use of the language in many common situations of daily life, so contextualizing all elements explained in the first two parts. Thus, dialogue represents a way to see how the Italian language works and helps you to understand it. One of the take-home messages of this book is that you need to express your thoughts to formulate questions and answer tpossible requests. Always keep in mind that you are learning another communication system, which can be similar to your native tongue, yet also different.

When dealing with a new language, you have to get the basic structure of a sentence. After which you will add new elements, new words (adverbs first, nouns, and adjectives). To start this process correctly, it is necessary to start with grammar, which represents the base of the language "tower". However, grammar is not enough; it is only with words that you have the "bricks" to build the "tower". For this reason, the last part of the book is dedicated to the glossary, which has been divided into basic verbs and nouns that relate to a given topic.

Good luck on your language learning journey!

Section 1 – Basis of Grammar

1.1 The Italian Alphabet: Spelling and Sounds

Italian is defined as a transparent language, which means that each letter corresponds to a sound—rather than in English, where each letter may correspond to many different sounds. This means that reading Italian is quite easy—you just have to follow some rules.

1.1.1 The Italian alphabet

Letters of the alphabet don't give pronunciation rules, but there are tools to spell out words:

A (**a** like the **a**rm)

B (**bi** like **bi**g)

C (**ci** like **c**heat)

D (**di** like **di**slike)

E (**e** like **e**nd)

F (**effe** like **eff**ect)

G (**gi** like **gy**m)

H (**acca** like **acc**ount)

I (i like impress)

L (elle like element with double l)

M (emme like emmer)

N (enne like energy with double n)

O (o like ostrich)

P (pi like pig)

Q (qu like question)

R (erre like erect with double r)

S (esse like essential)

T (ti like tip)

U (u like put)

V (vu like wurst)

Z (zeta like zest and tap)

Remember: J, W, X, and Y don't exist in the Italian alphabet; if there are words with these letters, it means they are foreign words that have become part of the language.

While spelling, Italian people add the names of cities, as *A come Ancona* (A as Ancona), *B come Bologna* (B as Bologna), *C come Cagliari* (C as Cagliari), etc.

1.1.2 The Italian sounds

As mentioned, letters of the alphabet don't help so much with the pronunciation of letters, especially when they are combined.

1.1.2.1 Vowels

There are two types of vowel pronunciation in Italian: open and closed, and this literally depends on your mouth. Here are some examples:

A is always open and sounds like the a in the word fast.

I is always closed and sounds like the double "ee" in English words, such as feet.

U is always closed as well, and it sounds like the double "oo" in English words, such as f**oo**t.

Instead, E and O can be both open or closed. The different use is linked to different Italian regions and dialects.

E is closed and sounds like the a in s**ai**l, and when it is open, it sounds like the e in s**e**nd.

O is closed and sounds like the o in **o**pen, and when it is open, it sounds like the o in p**o**licy.

If you are thinking about how to recognize when they are open or not, don't worry. Time will help you, and also because the different use is linked to Italian regions and dialects. The most important difference, which is used in the same way for the whole country, is between È and E. The first one is open and corresponds to the English "is" (the third singular person of the verb to be - *essere*). It always has the stress to stand out from E, which means "and", and always has a closed sound.

<u>1.1.2.2 Consonants</u>

Most of the consonants sound as they are spelled, or read the same as in English. However, this does not happen with C, G, S, and Z.

The sounds of C and G depend on the vowel they come before, for example:

With E and I, the C sounds like the c in **ch**ase, while A, O, and U sound like the c in **c**astle.

With E and I, the G sounds like the g in **g**entle, while A, O, and U sounds like the g in **g**ap.

The sounds of S and Z depend on their position within the word, for example:

S sounds like the s in **r**ise if it's in between two vowels, and like the s in **s**treet when it comes before a consonant

Z sounds like the ds in a**dds** when the word starts with z; otherwise, it sounds like the ts in cu**ts**.

1.1.2.3 Combined sounds

The letters "c" and "g" change sound if they come before "h" and "s" before "c".

"ch" sounds like the "k" in **k**ey.

"gh" sounds like the "gu" in **gu**ilty.

"sc" sounds like the "sh" in **sh**ot.

There are also:

"gn" sounds like the "yo" in can**yo**n.

"gl" sounds like the "lli" in mi**lli**on.

1.2 Numbers, Days of the Week and Months

1.2.1 Numbers

To learn Italian numbers easily, you have to be careful while memorizing the ones that are completely different.

1.2.1.1 Cardinal Numbers

From zero to sixteen, they are completely different from each other.

0 zero

1 uno

2 due

3 tre

4 quattro

5 cinque

6 sei

7 sette

8 otto

9 nove

10 dieci

11 undici

12 dodici

13 tredici

14 quattordici

15 quindici

16 sedici

From seventeen to eighteen, you have to think about "dicia" as ten, plus the following number:

17 diciasette

18 diciotto

19 diciannove

Tens are:

20 venti

30 trenta

40 quaranta

50 cinquanta

60 sessanta

70 settanta

80 ottanta

90 novanta

If you want to say 21, 31, etc., and 28, 38, etc., you have to take off the final "a" and add "uno" or "otto". For example, ventuno or novantotto. For all the others, simply add the number after the ten. For example, trentadue, quarantatre, cinquantaquattro, sessantacinque, settantasei, ottantasette, etc.

You then have:

100 cento

1000 mille

It is simple going from one hundred, two hundred, three hundred, etc.; it is enough to add the number before "cento". For example, 500 is cinquecento (as the famous Italian car).

To go from one thousand, you do the same, but be careful: "mille" is used only for one thousand. In fact, from two thousand, you have to use "mila". For example, four thousand is quattromila.

1.2.1.2 Ordinal Numbers

From 1st to 10th, they are completely different from each other.

1st primo

2nd secondo

3rd terzo

4th quarto

5th quinto

6th sesto

7th settimo

8th ottavo

9th nono

10th decimo

From 11th, you simply add "esimo" at the end of the number by taking off its final vowel.

11th undicesimo

12th dodicesimo

13th tredicesimo

14th quattordicesimo

15th quindicesimo

20th ventesimo

and so on.

1.2.2 Days of the Week

The Italian days of the week come from Ancient Roman culture; "dì" stands for "day" and is another word for "giorno".

LUNEDÌ Monday

giorno della luna – day of the Moon

MARTEDÌ Tuesday

giorno di Marte – day of Mars

MERCOLEDÌ Wednesday

giorno di Mercurio – day of Mercury

GIOVEDÌ Thursday

giorno di Giove – day of Jupiter

VENERDÌ Friday

giorno di Venere – day of Venus

SABATO Saturday

giorno dei Saturno – day of Saturn

DOMENICA Sunday

giorno del Signore – day of Christ (from the Latin "Dominus")

All days can be plural, except Sunday, which is feminine, and they are all masculine (later, you'll see how to manage masculine and feminine, singular and plural).

1.2.3 Months

This is an easy part as they are very similar to the English ones.

GENNAIO January

FEBBRAIO February

MARZO March

APRILE April

MAGGIO May

GIUGNO June

LUGLIO July

AGOSTO August

SETTEMBRE September

NOVEMBRE November

DICEMBRE December

1.2.4 Dates

To express the date in Italian, it is not necessary to use first, second, third, etc. It works with one, two, three, etc. For example:

Today is September 23rd.

Oggi è il 23 di settembre.

Italians just use the cardinal number, plus "di", which means "of" and the month. The only exception is the first day of the month, where they use "primo" (first) too.

1.3 Articles

In Italian, as mentioned, names can be masculine or feminine. Gender can be recognized by the final vowel of the word ("o" for masculine and "a" for feminine), but there are also confusing cases, and so articles are the perfect tool to know if a word is masculine or feminine. Thus, a good way to learn words in Italian is to memorize words together with the corresponding article.

1.3.1 Definite articles

These are divided into masculine and feminine, and also into singular and plural. But the translation in English will be "the" for each one.

Masculine singular articles are: IL and LO.

Masculine plural articles are: I (for "il") and GLI (for "lo").

Feminine singular articles are: LA.

Feminine plural articles are: LE.

You might ask why there are two articles for masculine. This depends on how a word begins. If a word starts with "s" and a consonant, with "z", "gn", or a vowel, you have to use "lo". In this last case, "lo" loses its "o". In the spoken language, this will produce a sole sound, and in the written language, you will have to put an apostrophe instead of the "o"; for example, "lo albero" (the tree) will be "l'albero". The same will happen with feminine words starting with a vowel; for example, "la oca" (the goose) will be "l'oca".

The sole sound occurs only with singular names and articles, so "gli" and "le" won't ever lose their "i" and "e", and so the sound will be differentiated between the article and the name.

Their use has essential differences in English. First of all, Italian uses articles before a possessive (la mia casa, my home), and before the name of a continent, nation, and region, but not before a city. Another important difference is the use of the plural. In English, if you have to say that you like oranges, for example, you won't ever use "the oranges" if you are talking about oranges in general, not about specific ones. Instead, Italian will use it because names always come together with their articles.

1.3.2 Indefinite articles

These are divided into masculine and feminine, as definite ones, but they have only the singular form, like in English. The translation in English will be "a" or "an" for each one.

Masculine articles are: UN and UNO.

Feminine article is: UNA.

Again, you might wonder when to use "uno"; now the answer is easier: when you use "lo". As for definite articles, you will have a sole sound, and when the word that follows "uno" and "una" begins with a vowel—but only "una" will switch the "a" with the apostrophe; for example, "uno albero" (a tree) will be "un albero" and "una oca" (the goose) will be "un'oca".

1.4 Gender and Number

You are now ready to go deeper into how names and adjectives change, passing from masculine to feminine forms and vice-versa.

1.4.1 Gender

As previously stated, generally speaking, you can recognize if a word is masculine or feminine if it ends, in the singular, with "o" or "a". However, Italian also has words that end in "e". For this reason, it is crucial to learn words with their articles because it leaves no doubts about the gender.

The general rule identifies words with "o" as masculine and "a" as feminine; so, if you have to talk about a male cat, you will say "il gatto"; while you will say "la gatta" for a female cat.

Some names further change form when changing gender, as so in English, like:

il padre (the father)

la madre (the mother)

il marito (the husband

la moglie (the wife)

il fratello (the brother)

la sorella (the sister)

il toro (the bull)

la mucca (the cow)

Words that do not change are "il/la cantante" (the singer), "il/la parente" (the relative), and il/la nipote (nephew, niece, granddaughter, grandson). Words that change their meaning depending on the gender are "il porto" (the harbor), "la porta" (the door), "il fine" (the scope), and "la fine" (the end).

Furthermore, there are groups of words that belong to masculine or feminine. As mentioned, the days of the week are all masculine, except "domenica", but the names of trees, months, mountains, seas, rivers, and lakes are all masculine, too, while fruits, continents, states, regions, and islands are all feminine.

1.4.2 Number

If you have to transform a word from its singular to its plural form, you will have an easy job. In fact, all masculine words change their last vowel into an "i" and all feminine words into "e". For example, "il problema" will become "i problemi", and "la casa" will become "le case". All words ending in "e" will have an "i" at the end, and it doesn't matter if it is masculine or feminine—"l'informazione" will be "le informazioni" as "lo studente" will be "gli studenti". Moreover, words ending in "tà", usually feminine words, do not change; for example "la città" and "le città" (the city and the cities), as well as foreign words like "la foto" and "le foto" (the photo and the photos), "il video" and "i video", and "lo sport" and "gli sport". Don't forget the word "auto", which is a very common word used instead of "macchina", meaning "car".

When it comes to switching from singular to plural, there is also an aspect related to how their sounds change, too. As explained, "ch" makes the sound "k", and "gh" sounds like "gu" in guilty; this happens when it is together with "e" or "i". You also know that "c" sounds like "k" together with "a", "o", and "u" as you know that "g" sounds like "g" in garage. This means that you could have some problems while making the plural of words ending in "o", which is supposed to become "i" and ending in "a", which is then supposed to become an "e".

If you have to do the plural of a masculine word ending in "co", like "casco" (helmet), you have to consider that the "c" has the sound of "k"; thus, when you change the "o" with the "i" to make the plural, you will have to add an "h" to obtain the same sound because "ci" doesn't sound like "ki", but as "che" in cheap. For the same reason, with words ending in go, for the masculine plural, it is necessary to add an "h" after "g". If you have to do the feminine plural of words ending in "ca" or "ga", so when you have to switch the "a" with an "e", it will be the same. For example, "amica" (feminine friend) will be "amiche" (feminine friends) and "bottega" (small shop) will become "botteghe".

1.5 Prepositions

This topic is one of the most important of any language you want to learn. In fact, prepositions give roles to a word in a sentence. By using one of them, you give a particular meaning to that word depending on what you want to say. For example:

I am talking to you.

I am talking about you.

The sentence is the same except for "to" and "about". So, the first one uses "to" because it focuses on the person the narrator is talking to; the second one, "about", introduces the argument the narrator is talking about.

1.5.1 An overview of prepositions

As said, prepositions are a very important topic, but also complex. So, you will proceed step by step. Here is the list of Italian prepositions with a translation so that you have a general framework:

DI (of) - A (to) - DA (from) - IN (in) - CON (with) - SU (on, about) - PER (for) - FRA/TRA (between).

1.5.2 Prepositions and definite articles

The use of definite articles in Italian is different from English, especially because Italians use them everywhere. And, of course, they use them together with prepositions, too. When the prepositions "di", "a", "da", "in", and "su" come with a definite article, they become one word. Results of compositions are as follow:

DI+IL = del

DI+LO = dello

DI+LA = della

DI+I = dei

DI+GLI = degli

DI+LE = delle
A+IL = al
A+LO = allo
A+LA = alla
A+I = ai
A+GLI = agli
A+LE = alle
DA+IL = dal
DA+LO = dallo
DA+LA = dalla
DA+I = dai
DA+GLI = dagli
DA+LE = dalle
IN+IL = nel
IN+LO = nello
IN+LA = nella
IN+I = nei
IN+GLI = negli
IN+LE = nelle
SU+IL = sul
SU+LO = sullo
SU+LA = sulla
SU+I = sui
SU+GLI = sugli
SU+LE = sulle

It is not hard to use them; you just have to think.

1.5.3 Prepositions of time

These prepositions are used to introduce a time when something happened.

Use the preposition "a" with months (a marzo - in March), meals (a colazione - at breakfast, a pranzo - at lunch, a cena - at dinner), and periods (a Natale - at Christmas). To say the time, you have to use "a" again but together with the article (alle 5 - at 5 o'clock).

You use "in" with seasons (in estate - in summer) and with years, but plus the article (nel 1985 - in 1985).

Days do not need any preposition (lunedì - on Monday).

1.5.4 Prepositions of place

These prepositions refer to the position of something or someone.

Generally speaking, it is not so different from English; "a" translates "to" and is used for a movement toward a place, while "in" is used when inside a place. Some common verbs have a special use of the preposition, such as "stare" (to stay), which can be used both with "in" and "a", "partire" (to leave), which goes with "for", and "camminare" (to walk) that is followed by "verso" (towards), which is not a real preposition.

Things get more complicated with two verbs: "vivere" (to live) and "andare" (to go). If they are followed by cities, towns, villages, and small islands, the right preposition to use is "a". For example, "vado/vivo a Milano" - I go to Milan/in Milan. However, if continents, nations, regions, and big islands come after, you have to use "in". For example, "vado/vivo in Germania" - I go to Germany/in Germany.

1.6 Personal subject and direct pronouns

1.6.1 Personal subject pronouns

As in English, these work as a replacement of the subject, who does the action. Such as in the sentence, "Peter eats a piazza," the person who does the action is Peter, and he can be replaced by "he". Here is the Italian translation of personal subject pronouns:

IO = I
TU = YOU
LUI = HE
LEI = SHE
NOI = WE
VOI = YOU
LORO = THEY

As you can see, there is nothing to translate "it", and this is because Italians have a gender for things and animals, too, so they use "lui" for males and "lei" for females.

Moreover, remember that to be polite and formal, when speaking to a Mr (un signore) or a Mrs (una signora), Italian uses the 3rd singular person "lei" to refer both to a man or a woman.

So, "what's your name?" (informal) is: "come ti chiami?" and (formal) "come si chiama?"; "are you Mr. Rossi?" which is formal, is "Lei è il signor Rossi?"

1.6.2 Personal direct pronouns

As in English, they work as a replacement of the object, which is what undergoes the action. Such as in the sentence "Peter eats a pizza," the thing which undergoes the action is pizza, and it can be replaced by "it". Here are the Italian translations of personal direct pronouns:

MI = ME
TI = YOU
LO = HIM
LA = HER
CI = US
VI = YOU

LI = THEM (if referring to a "male" group)

LE = THEM (if referring to a "female" group)

This is only a direct translation of personal object pronouns. Later, their function in a sentence, together with other elements, is discussed. Right now, the only important thing to remember is that they always come before the verb.

1.7 Basic verbs: essere and avere

Essere (to be) and avere (to have) are the bases of each language and a good starting point for building sentences.

1.7.1. Essere

The use of essere is the same as "to be" in English, so it says more about people's appearances and professions, or an object's shape, color, size, etc.

IO SONO = I AM

TU SEI = YOU ARE

EGLI È = HE IS

ELLA È = SHE IS

ESSO/ESSA È = IT IS

NOI SIAMO = WE ARE

VOI SIETE = YOU ARE

ESSI/ESSE/LORO SONO = THEY ARE

Here, remember what was mentioned above regarding speaking Italian vowel sounds: "è" is the verb "to be" (corresponding to "is") and the sound is open, while "e" is a conjunction (corresponding to "and") and the sound is closed.

The expressions "there is" and "there are" are translated in Italian with "c'è" and "ci sono", where "c'" is the abbreviation of "ci", which means "there", "in that place".

1.7.2 Avere

The use of avere is the same as "to have" in English, so it refers to possessing something, someone (like relatives), and illnesses (like a headache).

IO HO = I HAVE

TU HAI = YOU HAVE

EGLI HA = HE HAS

ELLA HA = SHE HAS

ESSO/ESSA HA = IT HAS

NOI ABBIAMO = WE HAVE

VOI AVETE = YOU HAVE

ESSI/ESSE/LORO HANNO = THEY HAVE

Please note that the "h" in Italian does not have any sound; it is mute. So when speaking, there is no difference between "o" (or) and "ho" (I have) or "a" (to) and "ha" (has), or "anno" (year) and "hanno" (they have). However, when you write, you have to keep these differences in mind—even if it's one of the most common grammar mistakes (among Italians, too), people will understand you anyway.

1.7.3 Some different uses

Compared to English, there are some different uses of these two verbs.

1.7.3.1 Different uses of essere

These expressions, used in English with the verb "to be", are translated in Italian with "avere". You might find this strange; however, you just have to imagine that, if in English you would say, "I'm cold," like you are feeling it, in Italian, you "possess" it, as when you say that you have got stomachache!

To be hungry = avere fame

To be thirsty = avere sete

To be sleepy = avere sonno

To be in a hurry = avere fretta

To be afraid = avere paura

To be hot = avere caldo

To be cold = avere freddo

To be right = avere ragione

To be wrong = avere torto

Note that, in English, these expressions are made by "to be" plus the adjective, while in Italian, by "avere" plus the noun.

1.7.3.2 Different uses of avere

These expressions, used in English with the verb "to have", are translated in Italian with "fare" (to do/to make). In this case, you just have to think that you are doing something. For example, in English, you say, "I have a shower," because you are referring to the act of "doing" it; in Italian, you exactly "do" it as when you say that you do your homework! Other expressions are simply translated with a specific verb.

To have breakfast = fare colazione

To have lunch = pranzare

To have dinner = cenare

To have a holiday = fare una vacanza

To have a nap = fare un pisolino

To have a shower/bath = fare una doccia/un bagno

To have a swim = fare una nuotata

To have a good time/fun = divertirsi

You still have to learn how to use verbs and how they change for each person and tense, so don't worry! Soon you will be able to use any Italian verb properly.

1.8 Demonstrative and possessive adjectives

Introducing these elements will give you the tools to build a sentence.

1.8.1 Demonstrative adjectives

The use of these is the same as in English. The only difference is that there is not only a singular and a plural form, but you also have to be careful with the gender.

This = questo (for masculine) - questa (for feminine)

These = questi (for masculine) - queste (for feminine)

That = quel/quello (for masculine) - quella (for feminine)

Those = quei/quegli (for masculine) - quelle (for feminine)

As you can see, for that and those you have two forms for the masculine; it is not a problem, just follow the rules you have seen for articles. So, as you use "il", you will use "quel", and the use of "quello" is the same of "lo". Regarding rules about the apostrophe, use rules of the articles again both for "lo" and "la".

Keep in mind the English expression "what I see". For example, it is not translated in Italian with the corresponding word for "what"; you say "che cosa", but with "quello che vedo", where "che" is "that".

1.8.2 Possessive adjectives

When dealing with possessive adjectives, you focus on the person who has the "thing", and the person who owns it, like in English, but you also have to consider if the owned thing is masculine or feminine, and, of course, if it's singular or plural. However, remember that "his", "her", and "it" correspond to only one person, so one adjective. In this case, Italian does not make any difference. See below:

My = mio (masculine and singular), mia (feminine and singular), miei (masculine and plural), and mie (feminine and plural).

Your = tuo (masculine and singular), tua (feminine and singular), tuoi (masculine and plural), and tue (feminine and plural).

His/her/its= suo (masculine and singular), sua (feminine and singular), suoi (masculine and plural), and sue (feminine and plural).

Our = nostro (masculine and singular), nostra (feminine and singular), nostri (masculine and plural), and nostre (feminine and plural).

Your = vostro (masculine and singular), vostra (feminine and singular), vostri (masculine and plural), and vostre (feminine and plural).

Their = loro both for masculine and feminine, and both for singular and plural.

Here are some examples:

My dog = il mio cane (as "cane" is masculine).

My dogs = i miei cani.

His/her/its car = la sua macchina (as "macchina" is feminine).

Their house = la loro casa (as "macchina" is feminine).

Their houses = le loro case.

As you can see, every possessive adjective has the definite article beforehand; in Italian, it is mandatory, while in English, it's forbidden!

In Italian, it is not used when you speak about your family as a singular. For example: my brother will be "mio fratello", without the article. But my brothers will be "i miei fratelli", with the article.

1.9 Adverbs

In English, these are easy to recognize because they have the final part of the word in "ly" and they give further information about what is being done. If you say "you eat slowly," you want to say something more about eating. In Italian, "ly" is represented by "mente". Of course, to form an adverb, you have to start from the adjective, as in English. Here is how it works:

veloce (fast) = velocemente (fast) – in English, there is no difference between the adjective and the verb.

lento (slow) = lentamente (slowly).

regolare (regular) = regolarmente (regularly).

fortunato (lucky) = fortunatamente (luckily).

And so on. Please note that if the adjective ends with "e", making the adverbs it is lost, and if it ends in "o", it changes to "a".

Some adverbs do not come from an adjective, as in:

vicino (near), troppo (too/too much), là (there), qui (here), mai (ever/never), spesso (often), sempre (always), prima (before), and dopo (after).

1.10 Relative pronouns

These pronouns are used as in English, but in this case, Italian makes things a bit less complicated. In fact, there is no difference between objects and people; you will not have to think about whether the relative pronoun is replacing a thing or a person.

Before starting, you need to understand what a relative pronoun is:

The girl who is talking is my new classmate = In this sentence, WHO is the relative pronoun, and it works as the subject in the sentence "is talking", and it replaces "the girl".

The man (that) you saw yesterday is Peter's father = In this sentence, THAT is the relative pronoun, and it works as the object in the sentence "you saw" (you saw, who? the man...) and it replaces "the man".

Mark, whose brother attends your school, is coming to the party = In this sentence, WHOSE is the relative pronoun, and it works as "of who – possession" in the sentence "attends your school" and it replaces "the girl".

In the first and second cases, Italian uses CHE or QUALE. CHE never changes—it is always the same for masculine or feminine and singular or plural. Instead, QUALE never changes its form, but you have to put before it the correct definite article (IL for masculine singular; LA for feminine singular; I for masculine plural; LE for feminine plural; and LO and GLI are never used in this case).

In the last sentence, Italian uses QUALE again, but beforehand, you have to put DI plus the correct definite article, making the compound prepositions (DEL for masculine singular; DELLA for feminine singular; DEI for masculine plural; DELLE for feminine plural; and LO and GLI are never used in this case).

If you have to translate "to which", use QUALE again, but beforehand you have to put A plus the correct definite article, making the compound prepositions (AL for masculine singular; AL for feminine singular; AI for masculine plural; ALLE for feminine plural; and LO and GLI are never used in this case).

Please remember that the choice of the article depends on the gender and number of the replaced word. For example, "alla quale" = "to which" referring "to her", "ai quali" = "to which" referring "to them" (all males), etc. Of course, the same can be used with other prepositions, and this depends on what you want to say. For example, "for which" = per il/la/i/le quali, "on which" = sul/sulla/sui/sulle quali, etc.

There is another option that works without the article and only with the preposition, CUI. As it can be used only with prepositions, it will never replace the subject or object. For example: "whose" = del/della/dei/delle quali or DI CUI, "to which" = al/alla/ai/alle quali or A CUI, and so on.

1.11 Demonstrative and possessive pronouns

There is no difference between demonstrative and possessive adjectives and pronouns. Of course, pronouns come without a name after...

This is my laptop, that is yours.

Questo è il mio computer portatile, quello è tuo.

As you can see, "tuo" is a pronoun and it is perfectly the same as the adjective.

1.12 Interrogative pronouns

These pronouns are used to make questions, as in English. The only difference is that, in Italian, the preposition comes before the interrogative pronoun and not at the end of the sentence:

Where are you from?

Di dove sei?

First of all, note that "from" is translated with "di" and not "da". This is because to speak about the place of origin, Italian uses "di". Afterward, you can see that the preposition is before "dove" (where) and not at the end of the question.

Other interrogative pronouns are:

CHI = who

COME = how

QUANDO = when

PERCHÉ = why/because (there is no difference in Italian)

QUANTO/A = how much

QUANTI/E = how many

QUALE = what/which

CHE COSA/CHE = what

1.13 Indefinite adjectives and pronouns

Indefinite adjectives and pronouns are used to indicate a certain quantity of something or number of people or to refer to something or someone which is not determined.

1.13.1 Indefinite adjectives

To indicate a certain quantity, a non-specific number of something or people, English uses some, any, and no. Now, see their translations in Italian through some examples:

There are some oranges in the fridge - where "some" is the indefinite adjective.

In Italian, there are several ways to translate "some"; in this case, like "alcune", "delle", and "qualche", but you have to observe that "oranges" is a countable name, which is technically a name that can have a plural form. So, the translation will be:

Ci sono alcune/delle/arance in frigo - C'è qualche arancia in frigo.

In the sentence, "there is some sugar". The word sugar is uncountable (so it has only the singular form) and so the Italian translations for some are "un po'" (which is the abbreviation of "un poco" - a little) or "dello". So, the translation will be:

C'è un po'/dello zucchero.

To sum up, with the singular, you can use "un po'", "del/dello/della"; and with the plural, "alcuni/alcune", "dei/degli/delle" (according to the gender and the number of the noun they refer to), and qualche (which doesn't ever change and goes always with a singular name). These indefinite adjectives are the same when used in questions. A difference you may remember is that, usually, Italian doesn't use them in a negative sentence, so there is no translation for "any" or "no" when you want to say there is no quantity of what you are talking about.

For example, if you take the previous two examples and turn them into the negative form, you will have:

There are no oranges in the fridge/there aren't any oranges in the fridge - Non ci sono arance.

There is no sugar/there isn't any sugar - Non c'è zucchero.

As you can see, there is no indefinite adjective.

If you want to translate "no" not to speak about quantity, but to say "at all", you can use "nessuno" or "nessuna", and remember that the masculine form loses the final "o". For example:

Non c'è nessuno problema - there is no problem (at all).

Non c'è nessuna soluzione - there is no solution (at all).

1.13.2 Indefinite pronouns

These pronouns in English are simply obtained by putting together "some", "any", and "no" with "thing" or "body"/"one" when they refer to people. In Italian, these pronouns have different forms and different uses, actually quite complicated ones—but don't worry; it is possible to learn them focusing on their translation. Some of them change according to gender and number, others only regarding the number, and others never change. Now you will go through them one by one.

Alcuno, alcuna, alcuni and alcune.

As you can see, this changes according to the gender and number; it refers both to things and people, and it translates "somebody"/"something" in the affirmative sentences, and "anybody"/"anything" or "nobody"/"nothing in the negative ones. But remember: It can work also as an adjective as you have already seen. An example:

Alcuni sono al mare oggi - Somebody is at the beach today.

C'è qualche problema? No, nessuno - Is there any problem? No, nothing.

Qualcuno, qualcuna, qualcuni and qualcune.

These also change according to the gender and number; they refer both to things and people, and it translates "somebody"/"something" in the affirmative sentences, and "anybody"/"anything" in the interrogative ones. It only works as a pronoun:

C'è qualcuno in casa? Si, c'è Maria - Is there anybody home? Yes, there is Maria.

È notte, e c'è qualcuno alla scuola. È strano - It's night, and there's someone at school. It's weird.

Nessuno, nessuna

These can be only masculine or feminine, and it translates "anybody"/"anything" or "nobody"/"nothing in the negative sentences. It can also work as an adjective, as you have already seen.

Non c'è nessuno a casa – There is nobody at home/there isn't anybody at home.

Lastly, there are indefinite pronouns, which have only one form for both masculine and feminine and singular and plural and are used for things. These are "qualcosa" and "niente".

C'è qualcosa da bere? No, non c'è niente – Is there anything to drink? No, there is nothing/there isn't anything.

Please note that "niente" has a negative value, but in Italian, you always have to use "non" to make the negative form of the verb too.

Other forms are:

"ciascuno" and "ciascuna", that don't have the plural form and translates "each one" or "each ones"; "ognuno" and "ognuna", that don't have the plural form too and are used to translate "everything" or "everybody"; and "chiunque" that only has one form and is used for people to translate "anybody" when, in English, it is used in affirmative sentences. The correspondent form of "anything" used in the same case will be "qualsiasi cosa".

Lui ama chiunque – He loves anybody.

Lui ama qualsiasi cosa – He loves anything.

There are other forms, but the above is enough for now, as this is all you need to start speaking Italian!

1.14 Quantifiers

You have seen how to express an indefinite quantity, but you still need to learn how to express a big or small amount of something. In English, there are many ways to say it, so now see translations starting from English. Before starting, consider that what is uncountable in English, is the same in Italian, except for:

advice (consiglio), accommodation (alloggio), furniture (mobile), information (informazione), news, (notizia) and hair (capello).

All of these words have a plural form in Italian.

Poco and poca – little (used for what you can't count).

Pochi and poche – few (used for what you can count).

Molto/tanto and molta/tanta – much (used for what you can't count).

Molti/tanti and molte/tante – many (used for what you can count).

Troppo and troppa – too much (used for what you can't count).

Troppi and troppe – too many (used for what you can count).

Of course, in addition, it is not possible to count singular forms with words, and with plural forms, which are possible to count, you always have to pay attention to the gender of the name that follows.

For example, if you want to say "there is too much sugar in this cake and few apples," you have to consider that sugar is uncountable, while apples are countable. Furthermore, "sugar" is "zucchero", which is a masculine singular word, and "apples" is "mele", a feminine plural word.

The translation will be:

C'è troppo zucchero in questa torta e poche mele.

1.15 Comparatives and superlatives

1.15.1 Comparatives

As in English, comparatives are used to compare two elements with an adjective in order to say that one element is as, less, or more than the other one.

1.15.1.1 Comparative of equality

This uses the word "come" – as – after the adjective:

"Mario è alto come Luca" – Mario is as tall as Luca.

1.15.1.2 Comparative of minority

This uses the word "meno" – less – before the adjective and "di" after it (which stands for "than" in English):

"Mario è meno alto di Luca" – Mario is less tall than Luca.

1.15.1.3 Comparative of majority

This uses the word "più" – more – before the adjective and "di" after it (which stands for "than" in English):

"Mario è più alto di Luca" – Mario is taller than Luca.

Also, in Italian, "buono"– good – and "bad" – cattivo – are irregular.

buono – migliore.

cattivo – peggiore.

1.15.2 Superlatives

As in English, superlatives are used to compare a small unit to a group. In Italian, they are formed by adding the definite article before the adjective:

"Mario è il più alto della classe" – Mario is the tallest of the class.

"Laura è la meno simpatica delle sorelle" – Laura is the less nice of the sisters.

"Nicola è il migliore, e Paolo il peggiore" – Nicola is the best, and Paolo is the worst.

Section 2 – Verbal System

Before going through all the moods and tenses of Italian verbs, you have to focus on the three conjugations that represent the basic elements to get the pattern of each declension.

The moods are: indicativo, condizionale, congiuntivo, and imperativo. In this book, you won't learn about congiuntivo, which is the most complicated one, as it is studied at a higher level.

Italian has three conjugations: ARE, ERE, and IRE. Verbs with these endings are the infinitive forms—what English expresses by TO plus the base form of the verb. What makes these three conjugations different are the vowels A, E, and I before "re"; these vowels characterize the verbs in each mood and tense.

2.1 Present tenses

There are two present tenses in Italian used in the indicative mood: "presente indicativo" and "stare" plus "gerundio". To link them to a general translation in English, you can think that "presente indicativo" corresponds to "present simple" and "stare" plus "gerundio" is the "present continuous" where "stare" is the verb "to be" and gerundio is the "ing form". The way they are used in Italian is a bit different, but you will start from their construction.

2.1.1 Presente indicativo

Just like English, in Italian, you have to start from the infinitive form; if English takes "to" off before the verb and adds subjects in its place, Italian removes "are", "ere", and "ire" and changes them with an ending that is different for each person (and this is why it is not necessary to use the subject before the verb). Start from the first conjugation, taking "amare" - to love as an example:

Io AMO, tu AMI, egli/ella AMA, noi AMIAMO, voi AMATE, loro AMANO.

As you can observe, the vowel "a" tags this first conjugation (except for "io" and "tu"), and the first part of the verb "am" never changes.

Now see how it works with the second and third conjugation, which are alike.

"scrivere" - to write:

Io SCRIVO, tu SCRIVI, egli/ella SCRIVE, noi SCRIVIAMO, voi SCRIVETE, loro SCRIVONO.

"partire" - to leave:

Io PARTO, tu PARTI, egli/ella PARTE, noi PARTIAMO, voi PARTITE, loro PARTONO.

As you can note, the vowels "e" and "o" tag the second and the third conjugation (except for "tu" and "noi", which is the same for all conjugations), and the first part of the verbs "scriv" and "part" never change.

As you have seen for the plural form, you have to think again about sounds; if you take a verb ending in "care" or "gare", you will see that with the person "tu", you have to make some changes to maintain the sound. For example:

the verb "giocare" - to play - cannot be "tu gioci" because this will be the sound of the "c" in "church" and it is not the same as the "c" in giocare, which sounds like the "c" in "castle". For this reason, you should add an "h" after the "c" and it will be "tu giochi".

Unfortunately, there are many irregular verbs. Below are the most common ones:

"andare" - to go

Io VADO, tu VAI, egli/ella VA, noi ANDIAMO, voi ANDATE, loro VANNO

"bere" - to drink

Io BEVO, tu BEVI, egli/ella BEVE, noi BEVIAMO, voi BEVETE, loro BEVONO

"dare" - to give

Io DO, tu DAI, egli/ella DÀ, noi DIAMO, voi DATE, loro DANNO

"dire" - to say/to tell

Io DICO, tu DICI, egli/ella DICE, noi DICIAMO, voi DITE, loro DICONO

"fare" - to do

Io FACCIO, tu FAI, egli/ella FA, noi FACCIAMO, voi FATE, loro FANNO

"salire" - to go/come up

Io SALGO, tu SALI, egli/ella SALE, noi SALIAMO, voi SALITE, loro SALGONO

"sapere" - to know

Io SO, tu SAI, egli/ella SA, noi SAPPIAMO, voi SAPETE, loro SANNO

"uscire" - to go out

Io ESCO, tu ESCI, egli/ella ESCE, noi USCIAMO, voi USCITE, loro ESCONO

"venire" - to come

Io VENGO, tu VIENI, egli/ella VIENE, noi VENIAMO, voi VENITE, loro VENGONO

2.1.2 Stare plus gerundio

As this is made of two parts, you have to understand how they are formed. First of all, see the presente indicativo di "stare", which is irregular:

"stare" - to stay

Io STO, tu STAI, egli/ella STA, noi STIAMO, voi STATE, loro STANNO.

Gerundio is formed by adding "ando" for verbs in ARE, and "endo" for verbs in ERE and IRE to the fixed part of the verb.

amare - amando

scrivere - scrivendo

partire - partendo

2.1.3 How to use "presente indicativo" and "stare plus gerundio"

When introducing these tenses, a translation was given, and it was stated that the use is a bit different. Now, you will see how.

"Stare plus gerundio" is only used when you have to speak about something that is happening at the moment, right now. Be careful— never use it for future actions; that is presente indicativo's job.

In fact, if you want to say, "I am having dinner with some friends tonight," you will have to say, "Ceno con alcuni amici stasera," and not "sto cenando." If the phrase is, "I am having dinner with some friends now," - "Sto cenando con alcuni amici ora," you will have two options. Sometimes, you can use the presente indicativo instead of "stare plus gerundio," but still to refer to something is happening now. For example: "Che cosa fai?" -- "Sto leggendo un libro"; this will be translated as "What are you doing?" - "I'm reading a book". But you could also use the form "che cosa stai facendo". In this case, it does not matter.

2.1.4 Adverbs of frequency

When the presente indicativo is used to speak about a habit in the present, as the present simple does in English, you may need adverbs of frequency that are words that indicate how something is done:

Always - sempre

Often - spesso

Usually - solitamente/di solito

Sometimes - qualche volta

Once - una volta

Twice - due volte (and so on)

Ever/never - mai

2.2 Past tenses

There are several past tenses in Italian: some belong to the indicative and others to other moods. Don't worry—you are not going to learn all of them here, but to begin, you will start with the indicative mood.

2.2.1 Passato prossimo

This is the most used tense to speak about the past, and so it's something you need to learn. Technically, you could compare it with the present perfect (I have gone, you have eaten, etc.), but its form and use is very different and the translation also corresponds to the past simple.

Firstly, you have to focus on the main difference: in English, you always use the verb "to have" to form compound tenses, while in Italian, you can use both "avere" and "essere" for the present indicativo. It sounds complicated, but it isn't. To understand what verbs go with "avere" and which ones go with "essere", you have to start from the concept of transitive and intransitive verbs—strange words but with easy practical meanings. Basically, a transitive verb is a verb that has an object, something that answers the questions "who" or "what"; for example, in the sentences "Mary called Lucy" or "Mary made a cake," Mary is the subject, so she is making the action, and "Lucy" and "cake" are the objects as they answer the question "who" for "Lucy" and "what" for "a cake". On the contrary, intransitive verbs do not have an object; for example, in the sentence "Mary went to the park," nothing answers the questions "who" or "what", because "in the park" better answers the question of "where".

So, transitive verbs are compound with "avere", while intransitive verbs are compounded with "essere". Here are some example sentences:

Mary called/has called Lucy – Mary ha chiamato Lucy

Mary made/has made a cake – Mary ha fatto una torta

but Mary went/has gone to the park – Mary è andata al parco

Unfortunately, there are many intransitive verbs, which use "avere" instead of "essere". The most common are:

Camminare – to walk, viaggiare – to travel, lavorare – to work, cenare – to have dinner, piangere – to cry, dormire – to sleep – etc.

As you can see, after "avere" and "essere", there are "chiamato", "fatto", and "andata"; these are past participles, which in English, when regular, are formed by adding "ed" at the end of the verb.

In Italian, regular past participles are formed by adding ATO for verbs in ARE, UTO for verbs in ERE, and ITO for verbs in IRE to the fixed part of the verb:

"andare" becomes "andato"

"credere" becomes "creduto"

"dormire" becomes "dormito".

There is only one problem—many verbs have an irregular past participle. The most common are:

"to open": aprire – aperto

"to drink": bere – bevuto

"to ask": chiedere – chiesto

"to close": chiudere – chiuso

"to run": correre – corso

"to say/tell": dire – detto

"to be": essere – stato

"to do/make": fare – fatto

"to read": leggere – letto

"to put": mettere – messo

"to die": morire – morto

"to be born": nascere – nato

"to lose": perdere – perso

"to take": prendere – preso

"to answer": rispondere – risposto

"to break": rompere – rotto

"to chose": scegliere – scelto

"to get down": scendere – sceso

"to write": scrivere – scritto

"to switch off": spegnere – spento

"to spend": spendere – speso

"to happen": succedere – successo

"to see/watch": vedere – visto

"to come": venire – venuto

"to won": vincere – vinto

"to live": vivere – vissuto

When there are lists of irregular verbs, it is common to think "No way!" but consider that many of the verbs above are irregular in English, too! So, just keep calm and try to learn them two by two or try to form phrases with them and take your time.

There is something more to know about the past participle in Italian. In fact, if you observe the example above, you can see that the past participle changes depending on the person whom it is referring to:

"Mary ha fatto una torta" but "Mary è andata al parco", where "fatto" ends with "o" and "andata" with "a". This is because when you use verb "essere" to make compound forms of the verbs, the past participle takes the number and gender of the person who is making the action, the subject; this never happens when you use "avere" to make compound tenses. So:

"Io ho/tu hai/egli/ella ha/noi abbiamo/voi avete/loro hanno FATTO una torta."

"Io sono/tu sei/egli/ella è ANDATO-ANDATA al parco."

"Noi siamo/voi siete/loro sono ANDATI-ANDATE al parco."

2.2.2 Imperfetto

This tense does not exist in English, so it is not possible to give a translation; you will see later how to use past tenses in Italian compared to English. For the moment, just learn how to form it.

As for the presente indicativo or past participle, you always have to take the fixed part of the verb:

"to go": andare - io andavo, tu andavi, egli/ella andava, noi andavamo, voi andavate, loro andavano.

"to spend": spendere - io spendevo, tu spendevi, egli/ella spendeva, noi spendevamo, voi spendevate, loro spendevano.

"to leave": partire - io partivo, tu partivi, egli/ella partiva, noi partivamo, voi partivate, loro partivano.

As you can see, the fixed part of the verb never changes but also the final parts "vo", "vi", va", "vamo", "vate", and "vano"; the only thing that changes is the vowel between the fixed part of the verb (called the root) and the ending part of it (called the suffix). So, you have "a" for verbs in "are", "e" for verbs in "ere", and "i" for verbs in "ire". Easy, isn't it? So, to make it a bit harder, here are the irregular verbs:

"to be": essere - io ero, tu eri, egli/ella era, noi eravamo, voi eravate, loro erano.

"to do/make": fare - io facevo, tu facevi, egli/ella faceva, noi facevamo, voi facevate, loro facevano.

"to say/tell": dire - io dicevo, tu dicevi, egli/ella diceva, noi dicevamo, voi dicevate, loro dicevano.

"to drink": bere - io bevevo, tu bevevi, egli/ella beveva, noi bevevamo, voi bevevate, loro bevevano.

To learn them easier and faster, note that the only thing which changes is the root of the verb, the fixed part, except for "essere": "fare" becomes "fac-", "dire" becomes "dic-", and "bere" becomes "bev-".

The expressions "there was" and "there were" are translated in Italian with "c'era" and "c'erano", where "c'" is the abbreviation of "ci", which means "there", "in that place".

2.2.3 Stare plus gerundio

Now a quick look at the past version of "stare" plus gerundio. The form is the same seen for the present, except, of course, for the tense of "stare", which is used at the imperfetto:

Io STAVO, tu STAVI, egli/ella STAVA, noi STAVAMO, voi STAVATE, loro STAVANO plus amando, scrivendo or partendo. The translation corresponds to the past continuous:

Luca stava mangiando una pizza - Luca was eating a pizza.

2.2.4 Uses of passato prossimo, imperfetto, and stare plus gerundio

Before going through the uses of passato prossimo, imperfetto, and stare plus gerundio, it is important to know that there is another past tense called "passato remoto" that corresponds to the English past simple, but you won't study it for the moment. This tense is not used in the colloquial language, except for some regions in the south of

Italy and Tuscany. For this reason, you can use passato prossimo when referring to a concluded action in the past or an action that is something that has just finished and somehow still has connections with the present, but is over. You can also use passato prossimo to speak about what happened once or never.

Here are some examples:

Ieri sono andato al parco - Yesterday I went to the park (concluded action in the past).

Ho appena finito di mangiare - I have just finished eating (just concluded action).

Non sono mai stato a Londra - I have never been to London (something that never happened).

On the other hand, if the action in the past describes a habit in the past, something you used to do, imperfetto is the right tense. However, it is also used to describe an ongoing action in the past (where English would use past continuous), to speak about a certain state, description of a state of mind, or of how something or someone appeared, and when an action represents the cause of something else when it has a consequence.

Here are some examples:

Mentre Mary studiava, Peter leggeva - While Mary was studying, Peter was reading (two ongoing actions in the past).

Faceva freddo, ed io ero molto felice perché nevicava - It was cold, and I was happy because it was snowing (two descriptions - "was cold" and "was happy" - and one ongoing action in the past - "was snowing").

Ieri Mary aveva la febbre e così non è andata al lavoro - Yesterday Mary had a fever and so she didn't go to work ("aveva la febbre" is the reason whe she "didn't go to work").

As you can see, only ongoing actions are translated with the past continuous in English; the rest use the past simple. So, if you have to translate a past simple or present perfect from English to Italian, stop and think: if it is a description, a habit in the past, or an action that caused something else, use imperfetto!

As you have just seen, with an ongoing action, you use imperfetto, but you can use also the imperfetto of "stare" plus gerundio, which is the perfect correspondent of the past continuous in English. Take the previous example, where imperfetto expressed an ongoing action:

Mentre Mary studiava, Peter leggeva - While Mary was studying, Peter was reading.

In this sentence, there are two verbs at imperfetto, and both represent ongoing actions in the past; so, the sentence could also be, "Mentre Mary stava studiando, Peter stava leggendo".

The same for "nevicava in the following sentence: "Faceva freddo ed io ero molto felice perché nevicava" - It was cold and I was happy because it was snowing - could be "faceva freddo ed io ero molto felice perché stava nevicando". To sum up, if you need to express an ongoing action, which took place in the past, and that, in English, would use the past continuous, in Italian, you have two options: imperfetto and imperfetto of "stare" plus gerundio.

2.2.5 Past expressions and adverbs

As stated, passato prossimo translates both the past simple and present perfect; therefore, you can have it with:

Last - scorso/passato

Ago - fa

When - quando

While - mentre

Ever/never - mai

Just - appena

Already - già

Yet - ancora (only negative)

Lately - recentemente

So far - finora

There are also two prepositions associated in English with the present perfect: since and for. In this case, Italian does not use any past tenses, but the presente indicativo. For example:

In the sentence "I have known him since 2000/we were children/for 20 years," you don't have to use any past tense in Italian, only the present: "Lo conosco dal 2000/da quando eravamo bambini/da 20 anni." As you can see, both "since" and "for" are translated with the preposition "da" followed by "quando". If there is a verb introducing the past expression, "I have known" is "conosco", which is presente indicativo.

2.2.6 Trapassato prossimo

The name of this tense sounds scary, but it is not too complicated. Firstly, you have to know that it corresponds to the English past perfect, and, both in English and Italian, it is used to refer to an action that happened before another in the past. For example:

I had just ended my essay when I got the email and had to do another one. I was so sad!

Here, the action of "ending" happens before "getting the email".

To make this tense in Italian, consider that it is quite similar to passato prossimo, but it does not use the presente indicativo of "essere" or "avere". Now see the translation of the phrase above:

Avevo appena finito il mio saggio quando ho ricevuto una email e dovevo farne un altro. Ero così triste!

Here, "avevo appena finito" corresponds to "I had just ended", and it is trapassato prossimo.

2.3 Reflexive and indirect personal pronouns

2.3.1. Reflexive pronouns

These are: MI - myself, TI - yourself, SI - herself/himself/itself, CI - ourselves, VI - yourselves, and SI - themselves.

Their use is strictly linked to reflexive verbs.

2.3.2 Reflexive verbs

These are verbs whose meaning depends on the presence of reflexive pronouns. In fact, some of them have a meaning with the reflexive pronouns, but have a different one without it, while others only work with the reflexive pronoun. When a verb comes together with a reflexive pronoun, the latter comes before the verb. Here is an example:

lavarsi - to wash oneself

io mi lavo, tu ti lavi, egli/ella si lava, noi ci laviamo, voi vi lavate, loro si lavano

Of course, the tense of the verb changes based on the context.

There are four types of reflexive verbs:

1. The ones, like "lavarsi", where who is doing the action is doing it to himself/herself;

2. Verbs where who is doing the action isn't doing it to himself/herself, but to something that belongs to him. For example, "lavarsi i denti" - to brush "your" teeth;

3. Verbs where those people who are doing the action do so to each other, like "salurarsi" - to greet, noi ci salutiamo - we say goodbye (literally - I greet you, and you greet me).

4. The ones that only work as reflexive but do not have a reflexive meaning, like "arrabbiarsi": io mi arrabbio - I get mad.

There are many verbs belonging to group 1, and these change meaning, as stated before, if they come with or without a reflexive pronoun. Here is the list:

Alzare - to lift/alzarsi - to get up

Cambiare - to change/cambiarsi - to change clothes

Chiamare - to call/chiamarsi - to be named

Rompere - to break/rompersi - to break your bones.

Sbagliare - to make a mistake/sbagliarsi - to get wrong

2.3.3 Indirect personal pronouns

In Section 1, you saw direct personal pronouns—the ones that replace the object. Now you will see indirect personal pronouns, used in other cases—when a preposition precedes them. For example:

I do it for you - we came with her - they are speaking about him

Here "you", "her", and "him" are indirect personal pronouns because they come after a preposition. Before going on, note that even "him" in this sentence: "I told him" is an indirect personal pronoun because it works as it was "to him".

The following pronouns always come after a preposition:

me - te - lui - lei - noi - voi - loro.

I do it for you: "Lo faccio per te" (where "it" and "lo" are direct personal pronouns); we came with her: "Noi veniamo con lei"; they are speaking about him: "Loro stanno parlando di lui".

With the preposition "to", so "a", there two options:

I told him: "Io parlo a lui" - "Io gli parlo".

So, it is possible to use "a" plus the indirect personal pronouns you have seen to work after the preposition, or:

mi - ti - gli (a lui) - le (a lei) - ci - vi - gli

and they always come before the verb and do not use any preposition. See all the examples below:

You give me an advice: "Mi dai un consiglio".

I give you an advice: "Ti do un consiglio".

I give him an advice: "Gli do un consiglio".

I give her an advice: "Le do un consiglio".

You give us an advice: "Ci dai un consiglio".

I give you an advice: "Vi do un consiglio".

I give them an advice: "Gli do un consiglio".

2.3.4 Combined personal pronouns

Now, see what happens when you have to use both a direct personal pronoun and an indirect one.

In the sentence "I'm writing a letter to Mary," "a letter" is the object and "to Mary" is to whom; if you have to replace them with a personal pronoun, you will have: "it" and "to her", and the sentence will become: "I'm writing it to her."

In Italian: "Sto scrivendo una lettera a Maria."

Starting from the object "una lettera", you will have to use the direct personal pronoun "la" (as "lettera" is feminine and singular).

"La sto scrivendo a Maria."

Then, replace only "a Maria" using the indirect personal pronoun "le" (a lei – to her).

"Le sto scrivendo una lettera."

However, when you have to use them together, the indirect personal pronoun will go before the direct personal pronoun and will change their form becoming:

me – te – glie (both for "gli" and "le") – ce – ve – glie and the example sentence: "Sto scrivendo una lettera a Maria" becomes: "Gliela sto scrivendo."

Only "glie" becomes one word with the direct personal pronoun because the others keep being alone:

Lui sta scrivendo una lettera a me – He's writing a letter to me – me la sta scrivendo.

Io sto scrivendo una lettera a te – I'm writing a letter to you – te la sto scrivendo.

Io sto scrivendo una lettera a lui/a lei" - I'm writing a letter to him/to her - gliela sto scrivendo.

Lei sta scrivendo una lettera a noi - She's writing a letter to us - ce la sta scrivendo.

Io sto scrivendo una lettera a voi - I'm writing a letter to you - ve la sto scrivendo.

Io sto scrivendo una lettera a loro - I'm writing a letter to them - gliela sto scrivendo.

The last thing you have to know deals with personal pronouns and compound tenses. As stated, the past participle never changes with avere; this is not completely true as it changes when, with direct or combined personal pronouns, taking the gender and number of the direct pronoun. For example:

"Ho portato la macchina a Luca" - Gliel'ho portata, where "portata" agrees with "l'", which stands for "la" and refers to "macchina".

2.3.5 Verb "piacere"

This verb translates "to like", and if the meaning is the same, English and Italian build it in a very different way.

In English, the subject of "like" is the person who likes something or someone; in Italian, the subject is what is liked, and to understand who likes it, you have to say whom that thing or person is liked by specifically. It sounds like a turn of phrase, but look at the examples below:

I like chocolate - so "chocolate" is what is liked, and "I" represents who likes it. In Italian, the translation of this sentence is "mi piace la cioccolata," where "cioccolata" is the subject of the verb "piace" and "mi" stands for "to me". Another example:

She likes oranges - le piacciono le arance, where "arance" is the subject of the verb "piacciono" and "le" stands for "to her".

So, if the thing or person liked is singular, you have to use "piace"; if plural, it is "piacciono".

2.4 Imperative

The imperative is used to express orders to someone and usually to "you"; corresponding forms of "you" in Italian are "tu" (singular) and "voi" (plural).

"Tu" uses the 3rd person singular of presente indicative for verbs in ARE; "voi" uses the 2nd person plural of presente indicative:

mangiare -

magia! (tu)

mangiate! (voi)

While for verbs in ERE and IRE both "tu" and "voi" use the correspondent forms of presente indicativo, so the 2nd singular and plural persons:

spendere -

spendi! (tu)

spendete! (voi)

dormire -

dormi! (tu)

dormite! (voi)

There is another form of imperative that sounds more as an invitation, which is used in English with "let's" plus the verb. This, in Italian, corresponds to the 1st person plural of the presente indicativo:

andiamo! (noi) - let's go!

There are also forms to refer formally to Mr and Mrs, so "lei", but you won't see them this time because they use the congiuntivo, which you will study in upper levels.

However, there is still something you have to know about the imperativo; the position of personal pronouns in this mood.

In the sentence "tu scrivi una lettera a Maria," you know that "lettera" corresponds to the direct personal pronoun "la", and "a

Maria" to the indirect personal pronoun "le"; you also know that together they become "gliela". In all moods, these pronouns come before the verbs, except the imperativo and infinito.

gliela scrivi (presente inidicativo)

scrivigliela! (imperativo)

scrivergliela (infinito)

2.5 Future

2.5.1 Simple future

The use of this tense corresponds to the English "will" plus verb; as stated, the present continuous with a future value, in Italian, is given by the presente indicativo. Now see how to form it.

All verbs add "erò" for "io", "erai" for "tu", "erà" for "lui/lei", "eremo" for "noi", "erete" for "voi", and "eranno" for "loro":

io amerò, scriverò, partirò

tu amerai, scriverai, partirai

lui/lei amerà, scriverà, partirà

noi ameremo, scriveremo, partiremo

voi amerete, scriverete, partirete

loro, ameranno, scriveranno, partiranno

Until now nothing particularly hard.

However, there are verbs whose fixed part changes; otherwise, their sound will be weird:

"andare" (to go) becomes andr-

"avere" (to have) becomes avr-

"dovere" (to have to) becomes dovr-

"potere" (can) becomes potr-

"sapere" (to know) becomes sapr-

"vedere" (to see/to watch) becomes vedr-

"vivere" (to live) becomes vivr-

"bere" (to drink) becomes berr-

"tenere" (to keep) becomes terr-

"venire" (to come) becomes verr-

2.5.2 Compound future

As passato prossimo, this tense is compound, and so you will have to use the future simple of avere, for transitive verbs, and of essere, for intransitive verbs, plus the past participle. For example:

avrò, avrai, avrà, avremo, avrete, avranno mangiato

sarò, sarai, sarà andato/andata – saremo, sarete, saranno andati/andate

The use of "futuro composto", this is its name in Italian, is the same as "will" plus "have" plus "past participle" in English: When she will have arrived, I will cook the dinner.

It is used to speak about an action that will happen before another one in the future.

Actually, in Italian, there is another use, which expresses a supposition about something that could have happened. For example:

"Mary è in ritardo, avrà perso il treno." – "Mary is late; she would have missed the train."

2.6 Conditional

There are only two tenses here: present and past. The present corresponds to the English "would" plus "base form", "could", "may/might", and the past to "would/could/may/might have" plus "past participle". Both in English and Italian, the conditional is used formally or to express a possibility.

2.6.1 Present conditional

All verbs add "erei" for "io", "eresti" for "tu", "erebbe" for "lui/lei", "eremmo" for "noi", "ereste" for "voi", and "erebbero" for "loro":

io amerei, scriverei, partirei

tu ameresti, scriveresti, partiresti

lui/lei amerebbe, scriverebbe, partirebbe

noi ameremmo, scriveremmo, partiremmo

voi amereste, scrivereste, partireste

loro, amerebbero, scriverebbero, partirebbero

As you can see, it is very similar to the simple future; in fact, the verbs that change the fixed part of the future, do the same with the conditional.

Be careful! The 1st person plural "noi" differs from the simple future to the present conditional for one "m":

noi ameremo, scriveremo, partiremo - simple future

noi ameremmo, scriveremmo, partiremmo - present conditional

2.6.2 Past conditional

As all compound tenses, the past conditional also uses the present conditional of "avere" for transitive verbs, and "essere" for intransitive verbs, plus the past participle. For example:

avrei, avresti, avrebbe, avremmo, avreste, avrebbero mangiato

sarei, saresti, sarebbe andato/andata - saremmo, sareste, sarebbero andati/andate

2.7 Modal verbs: potere, volere, e dovere

These verbs are used in a language to determine the intention of an action: "potere" is used to ask or give permission, "volere" to express an intention or a desire or to speak about a possibility, and "dovere" for an obligation. If another verb follows, it has to be the infinitive form:

"posso aprire la finestra?" - can I open the window?

"voglio leggere" - I want to read

"devo lavorare" - I must/have to work

2.7.1 Potere

2.7.1.1 Presente indicativo

CAN – TO BE ABLE TO

Io posso, tu puoi, lui/lei può, noi possiamo, voi potete, loro possono

2.7.1.2 Passato prossimo e imperfetto

COULD – WAS/WERE – HAVE/HAS BEEN ABLE TO

Io ho, tu hai, lui/lei ha, noi abbiamo, voi avere, loro hanno potuto

Io potevo, tu potevi, lui/lei poteva, noi potevamo, voi potevate, loro potevano

2.7.1.3 Gerundio

BEING ABLE TO

potendo

HAVING BEEN ABLE TO

avendo potuto

2.7.1.4 Future

WILL BE ABLE TO

Io potrò, tu potrai, egli/ella potrà, noi potremo, voi potrete, loro potranno

WILL HAVE BEEN ABLE TO

Io avrò, tu avrai, egli/ella avrà, noi avremo, voi avrete, loro avranno potuto

2.7.1.5 Conditional

COULD – WOULD BE ABLE TO – MAY – MIGHT

Io potrei, tu potresti, egli/ella potrebbe, noi potremmo, voi potreste, loro potrebbero

WOULD HAVE BEEN ABLE TO

Io avrei, tu avresti, egli/ella avrebbe, noi avremmo, voi avreste, loro avrebbero potuto

2.7.2 Volere

2.7.2.1 Presente indicativo

TO WANT

Io voglio, tu vuoi, egli/ella vuole, noi vogliamo, voi volete, loro vogliono

2.7.2.2 Passato prossimo e imperfetto

WANTED -HAVE/HAS WANTED

Io ho, tu hai, egli/ella ha, noi abbiamo, voi avere, loro hanno voluto

Io volevo, tu volevi, egli/ella voleva, noi volevamo, voi volevate, loro volevano

2.7.2.3 Gerundio

(it is not used in English)

volendo

(it is not used in English)

avendo voluto

2.7.2.4 Future

WILL WANT

Io vorrò, tu vorrai, egli/ella vorrà, noi vorremo, voi vorrete, loro vorranno

WILL HAVE WANTED

Io avrò, tu avrai, egli/ella avrà, noi avremo, voi avrete, loro avranno voluto

2.7.2.5 Conditional

WOULD LIKE TO

Io vorrei, tu vorresti, egli/ella vorrebbe, noi vorremmo, voi vorreste, loro vorrebbero

WOULD HAVE LIKED TO

Io avrei, tu avresti, egli/ella avrebbe, noi avremmo, voi avreste, loro avrebbero voluto

2.7.3 Dovere

2.7.3.1 Presente indicativo

MUST - TO HAVE TO

Io devo, tu devi, egli/ella deve, noi dobbiamo, voi dovete, loro devono

2.7.3.2 Passato prossimo e imperfetto

HAD TO - HAVE/HAS TO

Io ho, tu hai, egli/ella ha, noi abbiamo, voi avere, loro hanno dovuto

Io dovevo, tu dovevi, egli/ella doveva, noi dovevamo, voi dovevate, loro dovevano

2.7.3.3 Gerundio

HAVING TO

dovendo

HAVING HAD TO

avendo dovuto

2.7.3.4 Future

WILL HAVE TO

Io dovrò, tu dovrai, egli/ella dovrà, noi dovremo, voi dovrete, loro dovranno

WILL HAVE TO

Io avrò, tu avrai, egli/ella avrà, noi avremo, voi avrete, loro avranno dovuto

2.7.3.5 Conditional

WOULD HAVE TO

Io dovrei, tu dovresti, egli/ella dovrebbe, noi dovremmo, voi dovreste, loro dovrebbero

WOULD HAVE HAD TO

Io avrei, tu avresti, egli/ella avrebbe, noi avremmo, voi avreste, loro avrebbero dovuto

2.8 CI and NE

Italian is the language of tiny words; in a sentence, you can hear many small words. In the previous part, you saw direct and indirect personal pronouns and how they can be combined, but there are two other small words, which are often used both in the common and formal language: "ci" and "ne".

2.8.1 Ci

You have already met this word; it can be a reflexive personal pronoun for "noi", a direct personal pronoun for "noi", or an indirect personal pronoun instead of "noi":

"Noi ci chiamiamo Marco e Marta." – Our names are Marco and Marta.

"Chi ci porta alla stazione?" – Who is taking us to the station?

"Ci piace il gelato" – We like ice cream.

However, sometimes it does not refer to "noi" but to "where", working as "there", in English, when you don't want to repeat the name of a place. Here are some examples:

"Hai mai visitato Siena?" – Have you ever visited Siena?

"Si, ci sono stato lo scorso anno." – Yes, I have. I was there last year.

Here "ci" stands for "Siena", and "ci" as a pronoun with a verb that is not imperative or infinitive, is placed before it.

"Sei stato al cinema di recente?" - Have you been to the cinema recently?

"No, non ci vado da molto tempo, ma vorrei andarci." - No, I haven't. I haven't gone (there) in a long time, but I would like to go (there).

In this sentence, both instances of "ci" stand for "cinema"; the first one comes with a verb at passato prossimo, and so it is before the verb, while the second one is together with the verb essere, at the end - "andare" is the infinitive. You can also see how Italian always uses "ci" even when English tends to imply it.

In fact, when speaking about "verbo essere" and "imperfetto", you have seen that the expressions "there is/there was" and "there are/there were" are translated in Italian with "c'è/c'era" and "ci sono/c'erano", where "c'" is the abbreviation of the "ci" currently being referenced.

<u>2.8.2 Ne</u>

This Italian word is frequently used and replaces "of something or someone". At first, it might seem complicated, but after reviewing some examples, the meaning will be clear:

"Buongiorno, Signora Rossi, quante mele vuole?" - Good morning, Mrs. Rossi, how many apples would you like?

"Buongiorno, ne vorrei dieci." - I would like ten (of apples), please.

"Che cosa è successo a Roma? Ne parlano da giorni." - What happened in Rome? They have been talking about it for days.

In the first sentence, "ne" replaces "apples", so "of them"—that English doesn't use—, while in the second sentence, it stands for "che cosa è successo", what happened, "about it".

Do you remember that mi, ti, gli/le, ci, vi, and gli change their form when they come together with a direct personal pronoun, becoming me, te, glie, ce, ve, and glie? The same happens when they come together with "ne". For example:

"Hai parlato del viaggio a Paolo?" - Have you talked to Paolo about the trip?

"Si, gliene ho parlato ieri sera." - Yes, I have. I talked to him (about it) last night.

Here, "glie" replaces "Paolo" (to him), and "ne" replaces "about the travel" (which English doesn't repeat).

2.8.3 Ci and Ne together

When "ci" comes together with "ne", it becomes "ce":

"quante palle ci sono nella scatola?" - How many balls are there inside the box?

"ce ne sono venti" - There are twenty (of balls, which is "ne" in Italian).

In this case, "ci" replaces "nella scatola" and becomes "ce" because it comes together with "ne".

"C'è del burro in frigo?" - Is there any butter in the fridge?

"No, non ce n'è." - No, there isn't any.

Here, again, "ci" replaces "nel frigo" and becomes "ce" because it comes together with "ne", which in turn loses the final "e" because of "è" after.

Section 3 – Grammar Exercises

This section is dedicated to some grammar exercises that will be very useful for you to test yourself on the topics learned in Sections 1 and 2.

3.1 Articles, gender, and number

3.1.1 Fill in the gaps with the correct definite or indefinite article:

a) A che ora arriva_____autobus?
What time does the bus arrive?

b) _____mattina di solito lavoro.
Usually, I work in the morning.

c) Paolo parla con_____suoi amici.
Paolo is speaking with his friends.

d) Manuele è_____studente diligente.
Manuel is a diligent student.

e) La Sig.ra Rossi è_____nostra insegnante di matematica
Mrs. Rossi is our Maths teacher.

f) _____problema è che non ho molti soldi, è _____periodo difficile.
The problem is that I don't have much money; it is a hard period.

g) Questo è_____esercizio molto facile.
This exercise is very easy.

h) Ho_____amica che vive a Londra.
I have got a friend who lives in London.

i) Domani ho_____esame di italiano.
Tomorrow, I have an/the Italian exam

j) _____libro di matematica è costoso.

This Maths book is very expensive.

3.1.2 Transform the following sentences into the plural form:

a) Il libro è interessante.

The book is interesting.

b) L'amica è felice.

The friend is happy.

c) La tazza di tè è sul tavolo.

The teacup is on the table.

d) La porta è chiusa.

The door is closed.

e) Il gioco nuovo è nella scatola.

The new game/toy is inside the box.

f) L'amico di Paolo è al lavoro.

Paolo's friend is at work.

g) La sorella di Marta è molto bella.

Marta's sister is very beautiful.

h) Lo studente è intelligente.

The student is smart.

i) La città è affollata.

The city is crowded.

j) Il bar è chiuso.

The bar is closed.

3.2 Subject and direct pronouns

3.2.1. Substitute the underlined words with the correct subject pronoun or find the implicit subject:

a) <u>Maria</u> canta sempre quando cucina. _____

Maria always sings while she cooks.

b) <u>Carlo e Anna</u> lavorano nello stesso ufficio. _____

Carlo and Anna work in the same office.

c) <u>Mi piace</u> molto la carne ma <u>preferisco</u> il pesce. _____

I like meat a lot, but I prefer fish.

d) <u>Il tavolo</u> è marrone. _____

The table is brown.

e) <u>Mia sorella ed io</u> viviamo con i nostri genitori. _____

My sister and I live with our parents.

f) <u>Luca</u> non conosce mio fratello. _____

Luca doesn't know my brother.

g) <u>Andate</u> spesso al cinema. _____

You often go to the cinema.

h) <u>Sono</u> tutti italiani in questo bar. _____

They are all Italian in this bar.

i) <u>Chi</u> ha già visto questo film? _____

Who has already watched this movie?

j) <u>Il gatto</u> di Marco si chiama Paolo, come mio padre. _____

Marco's cat name is Paolo, like my father.

3.2.2. <u>Substitute the underlined words with the correct object pronoun, then write the sentence again:</u>

a) La professoressa spiega <u>la lezione</u> agli studenti.

The professor explains the lesson to the students.

b) Oggi al mercato compro <u>le mele</u>.

Today, I am buying apples at the market.

c) Avete già spedito <u>gli inviti</u> per la festa?

Have you already sent the invitations to the party?

d) Ieri ho conosciuto le nuove amiche di mia sorella.

Yesterday, I met my sister's new friends.

e) Federico ha comprato i biglietti per il concerto.

Federico has bought the tickets for the concert.

f) Tua zia non scrive mai lettere.

Your aunt does not ever write letters.

g) Non capisco perché Paolo chiama sempre me.

I do not understand why Paolo always calls me.

h) Ieri ho visto tuo cugino alla fermata dell'autobus.

Yesterday, I saw your cousin at the bus stop.

i) Ho già invitato te.

I have already invited you.

j) Non vogliamo offendere voi.

We do not want to offend you.

3.3 Prepositions and verbs essere and avere

3.3.1 Fill in the gaps choosing the correct option:

a) Viaggio spesso 1. _____ lavoro perché 2. _____un agente 3. _____commercio. Mi vesto sempre elegante, 4. _____la giacca.

I often travel for work because I am a salesman. I always dress up in a suit.

1. a) per, b) di, c) sul

2. a) siete, b) sei, c) sono

3. a) per, b) di, c) nel

4. a) alla, b) con, c) della

b) Amo viaggiare perché posso prendermi una pausa 1. _____impegni d'ufficio. 2. _____Brasile ci vado ogni anno; mi piace camminare 3. _____strade piene 4. _____colori e gente.

I love traveling because I can take a break from office duties. I go to Brazil every year; I like walking through colored and crowded streets.

1. a) sulle, b) dagli, c) degli

2. a) in, b) per, c) a

3. a) per, b) sulle, c) nella

4. a) nel, b) a, c) di

    c) Mi sono trasferita 1. _____Italia 2. _____amore e ora 3. _____ a Roma 4. _____fare un corso di italiano.

I moved to Italy for love and now I am in Rome to attend an Italian course.

1. a) a, b) nell', c) in

2. a) all', b) di, c) per

3. a) siamo, b) è, c) sono

4. a) del, b) per, c) a

    d) 1. _____due fratelli e una sorella; Maria invece 2. _____solo un fratello e 3. _____molto simili.

I have got two brothers and one sister; Maria, instead, has only got one brother and they are very similar.

    e) 1. a) ho, b) abbiamo, c) avete

    f) 2. a) ha, b) hai, c) hanno

    g) 3. a) siamo, b) sono, c) siete

    h) Noi oggi 1. _____ delle cose da fare 2. _____centro; vieni 3. _____noi? C' 4. _____anche Giovanna.

Today, we have some things to do downtown; are you coming with us? Giovanna is coming too.

1. a) ho, b) abbiamo, c) avete

2. a) al, b) per, c) in

3. a) di, b) nel, c) con

4. a) è, b) ha, c) sono

3.4 Demonstratives and possessive adejectives

3.4.1 Fill in the gaps with the correct demonstrative adjective:

a) _____qui davanti è casa mia, _____in fondo alla strada è di mia sorella.

This is my house; the one at the end of the street is my sister's.

b) Non mi piace _____dolce.

I do not like this dessert.

c) Chi è_____ragazza seduta laggiù?

Who is that girl over there?

d) Ragazzi, _____qui è il mio amico Gianni.

Guys, this is my friend Gianni.

e) _____arco è l'Arco di Costantino.

This/that is Constantine's Arch.

f) Metto le scarpe da ginnastica o_____qui con il tacco?

Shall I wear tennis shoes or these high-heeled shoes?

g) _____è il mio libro di italiano, _____sul tavolo è il vostro.

This Italian book is mine; that one on the table is yours.

h) _____sono i miei genitori, Mario e Lucia.

These are my parents, Mario and Lucia.

i) _____è il volo per Milano.

This is the flight to Milan.

j) In_____classe dove siamo noi c'è la lezione di storia, _____studenti laggiù vanno alla lezione di filosofia.

In this class, where we are, there is a history class; those students over there are going to the philosophy class.

3.4.2 Fill in the gaps with the correct possessive adjective or pronoun:

a) Piero ci ha invitati a cena a casa_____.

Piero has invited us for dinner at his place.

b) Mi piace la_____borsa; dove l'hai presa?

I like your purse; where did you get it?

c) I_____genitori sono andati al cinema con _____fratello più piccolo.

My parents have gone to the cinema with my younger brother.

d) I_____amici mi aiutano sempre.

My friends always help me.

e) Ragazze, dove sono le_____amiche?

Girls, where are your friends?

f) La_____cultura è molto interessante perché siamo un popolo antico.

Our culture is very interesting because we are an ancient population.

g) Bambini, chi sono i_____genitori?

Kids, who are your parents?

h) La_____fortuna è stata che vi abbiamo incontrati.

Your luck was that we met you.

i) Mario e Susanna hanno cambiato macchina, la_____era molto vecchia.

Mario and Susanna changed car; theirs was very old.

j) Devo chiamare Giulia e dirle che la_____macchina è pronta.

I have to call Giulia and tell her that her car is ready.

3.5 Presente indicativo

3.5.1 Fill in the gaps with the correct form of the 1st person singular of the presente indicativo of verbs in brackets:

Ciao, 1. _____(chiamarsi) Thomas e 2. _____(essere) di Cracovia, ma 3. _____(abitare) a Roma da qualche mese. Per adesso 4. _____(vivere) in albergo ma 5. _____(cercare) casa. Da un po' di tempo 6. _____(guardare) gli annunci online ma non 7. _____(trovare) nulla di interessante. Domani 8. _____(andare) in agenzia e 9. _____(sperare) di trovare una persona che mi aiuti. 10. _____(avere) molta fiducia.

Hi, my name is Thomas, and I am from Cracow, but I have been living in Rome for a few months. By now, I am living in a hotel, but I am looking for a flat. For a while, I have been looking at real estate ads online, but I am not finding anything interesting. Tomorrow, I am going to a real estate agency, and I hope to find a person who can help me. I have a lot of faith.

3.4.2 Fill in the gaps with the correct form of the 3rd person singular of the presente indicativo of verbs in brackets:

Lui 1. _____(chiamarsi) Thomas e 2. _____(essere) di Cracovia, ma 3. _____(abitare) a Roma da qualche mese. Per adesso 4. _____(vivere)in albergo ma 5. _____(cercare) casa. Da un po' di tempo 6. _____(guardare) gli annunci online ma non 7. _____(trovare) nulla di interessante. Domani 8. _____(andare) in agenzia e 9. _____(sperare) di trovare una persona che lo aiuti. 10. _____(avere) molta fiducia.

He is Thomas, and he is from Cracow, but he has been living in Rome for a few months. By now, he is living in a hotel, but he is looking for a flat. For a while, he has been looking at real estate ads online, but he is not finding anything interesting. Tomorrow, he is going to a real estate agency, and he hopes to find a person who can help him. He has a lot of faith.

3.6 Past tenses

3.6.1 Fill in the gaps with the correct form of the passato prossimo or imperfetto of verbs in brackets:

Un pappagallo 1. _____(scappare) di casa: 2. _____(succedere) qualche giorno fa a Milano. I proprietari 3. _____(essere) molto tristi ma 4. _____(raccontare) la storia del pappagallo ai giornali. 5._____(chiamarsi) Ugo e per loro 6. _____ (essere) come un figlio. Lo 7. _____(lasciare) sempre libero in casa, ma un giorno il vento 8. _____(aprire) la finestra e lui 9. _____(volare) via. Fortunatamente lo 10. _____(trovare) pochi giorni dopo grazie all'aiuto di molti cittadini.

A parrot ran away from home: it happened some days ago in Milan. The owners were really sad, but they told the story of the parrot to the newspapers. Its name was Ugo, and it was like a son to them. They always let it fly free inside the house, but one day the wind opened the window, and it flew away. Luckily, they found it a few days after thanks to the help of many citizens.

3.7 Combined personal pronouns

3.7.1 Fill in the gaps with the correct combined personal pronoun:

a) Porto alla nonna la torta - _____ porto.

I am taking the cake to Grandmother.

b) Ci scrivi il tuo indirizzo? - _____ scrivi?

Can you write us your address?

c) Per Natale regalo un viaggio a Mario - _____ regalo per Natale.

For Christmas, I want to give a trip to Mario.

d) Chi vi presta la macchina per il viaggio? - _____ presta?

Who is going to lend you the car for the trip?

e) Hanno scritto un messaggio ai loro amici - _____ hanno scritto.

They have written a message to their friends/they have texted their friends.

f) Mi spieghi l'esercizio perché non l'ho capito? - _____ spieghi che non l'ho capito?

Can you explain to me the exercise because I did not understand it?

g) Avete chiesto a Paola se voleva venire anche lei? - _____ avete chiesto?

Have you already asked Paola if she wants to come as well?

h) Ti hanno già consegnato il pacco? - _____ hanno già consegnato?

Have they already delivered you the parcel?

i) Avete comprato i cioccolatini al nonno? - _____ avete comprati?

Have you already bought pralines for Grandfather?

j) Ho regalato una collana alla mia fidanzata - _____ ho regalata.

I gave my girlfriend a necklace as a gift.

3.8 Articles, gender, and number

3.8.1 Fill in the gaps with the correct definite or indefinite article:

a) A che ora arriva **l'**autobus?

b) **La** mattina di solito lavoro.

c) Paolo parla con **i** suoi amici.

d) Manuele è **uno** studente diligente.

e) La Sig.ra Rossi è **la** nostra insegnante di matematica

f) **Il** problema è che non ho molti soldi, è **un** periodo difficile.

g) Questo è **un** esercizio molto facile.

h) Ho **un'**amica che vive a Londra.

i) Domani ho **l'/un** esame di italiano.

j) **Il/un** libro di matematica è costoso.

3.8.2 Transform the following sentences into the plural form:

a) Il libro è interessante. **I libri sono interessanti**

Books are interesting

b) L'amica è felice. **Le amiche sono felici**

Friends are happy

c) La tazza di tè è sul tavolo. **Le tazze di tè sono sui tavoli**

Teacups are on the tables

d) La porta è chiusa. **Le porte sono chiuse**

Doors are closed

e) Il gioco nuovo è nella scatola. **I giochi nuovi sono nelle scatole**

New games/toys are inside the boxes

f) L'amico di Paolo è al lavoro. **Gli amici di Paolo sono al lavoro**

Paolo's friends are at work

g) La sorella di Marta è molto bella. **Le sorelle di Marta sono molto belle**

Marta's sisters are very beautiful

h) Lo studente è intelligente. **Gli studenti sono intelligenti**

Students are smart

i) La città è affollata. **Le città sono affollate**

Cities are crowded

j) Il bar è chiuso. **I bar sono chiusi**

Bars are closed

3.9 Subject and direct pronouns

3.9.1. Substitute the underlined words with the correct subject pronoun or find the implicit subject:

a) <u>Maria</u> canta sempre quando cucina. **Lei**

She

b) <u>Carlo e Anna</u> lavorano nello stesso ufficio. **Loro**

They

c) <u>Mi piace</u> molto la carne ma <u>preferisco</u> il pesce. **Io**

I

d) <u>Il tavolo</u> è marrone. **Esso**

It

e) <u>Mia sorella ed io</u> viviamo con i nostri genitori. **Noi**

We

f) <u>Luca</u> non conosce mio fratello. **Lui**

He

g) <u>Andate</u> spesso al cinema. **Voi**

You

h) <u>Sono</u> tutti italiani in questo bar. **Loro**

They

i) <u>Chi</u> ha già visto questo film? **Lui/lei**

He/she

j) <u>Il gatto</u> di Marco si chiama Paolo come mio padre. **Lui**

He (but, in English, "it" because it refers to a cat)

3.9.2. Substitute the underlined words with the correct object pronoun, then write the sentence again:

a) La professoressa **la** spiega agli studenti.

b) Oggi al mercato **le** compro.

c) **Li** avete già **spediti** per la festa?

d) Ieri **le** ho conosciute.

e) Federico **li** ha comprati per il concerto.

f) Tua zia non **le** scrive mai.

g) Non capisco perché Paolo **mi** chiama sempre.

h) Ieri **l'**ho visto alla fermata dell'autobus.

i) **Ti** ho già invitato.

j) Non **vi** vogliamo offendere.

3.10 Prepositions and the verbs essere and avere

3.10.1 Fill in the gaps choosing the correct option:

a) Viaggio spesso 1. _____ lavoro perché 2. _____un agente 3. _____commercio. Mi vesto sempre elegante 4. _____la giacca.

1. a) **per,** b) di, c) sul

2. a) siete, b) sei, c) **sono**

3. a) per, b) **di,** c) nel

4. a) alla, b) **con,** c) della

b) Amo viaggiare perché posso prendermi una pausa 1. _____impegni d'ufficio. 2. _____Brasile ci vado ogni anno; mi piace camminare 3. _____strade piene 4. _____colori e gente.

1. a) sulle, b) **dagli,** c) degli

2. a) **in,** b) per, c) a

3. a) **per,** b) sulle, c) nella

4. a) nel, b) a, c) **di**

c) Mi sono trasferita 1. _____Italia 2. _____amore e ora 3. _____ a Roma 4. _____fare un corso di italiano

1. a) a, b) nell', c) **in**

2. a) all', b) di, c) **per**

3. a) siamo, b) è, c) **sono**

4. a) del, b) **per**, c) a

d) 1. _____due fratelli e una sorella; Maria invece 2. _____solo un fratello e 3. _____molto simili.

e) 1. a) **ho**, b) abbiamo, c) avete

f) 2. a) **ha**, b) hai, c) hanno

g) 3. a) siamo, b) **sono**, c) siete

h) Noi oggi 1. _____ delle cose da fare 2. _____centro; vieni 3. _____noi? C' 4. _____anche Giovanna.

1. a) ho, b) **abbiamo**, c) avete

2. a) al, b) per, c) **in**

3. a) di, b) nel, c) **con**

4. a) **è**, b) ha, c) sono

Answer keys

3.11 Demonstratives and possessive adjectives

3.11.1 Fill in the gaps with the correct demonstrative adjective:

a) **Questa** qui davanti è casa mia, **quella** in fondo alla strada è di mia sorella.

b) Non mi piace **questo/quel** dolce.

c) Chi è **quella** ragazza seduta laggiù?

d) Ragazzi, **questo** qui è il mio amico Gianni.

e) **Quello/questo** arco è l'arco di Costantino.

f) Metto le scarpe da ginnastica o **queste** qui con il tacco?

g) **Questo** è il mio libro di italiano, **quello** sul tavolo è il vostro.

h) **Questi** sono i miei genitori, Mario e Lucia.

i) **Questo/quello** è il volo per Milano.

j) In **questa** classe dove siamo noi c'è la lezione di storia, **quegli** studenti laggiù vanno alla lezione di filosofia.

3.11.2 Fill in the gaps with the correct possessive adjective or pronoun:

a) Piero ci ha invitati a cena a casa **sua**.

b) Mi piace la **tua** borsa; dove l'hai presa?

c) I **nostri** genitori sono andati al cinema con il **nostro** fratello più piccolo.

d) I **miei** amici mi aiutano sempre.

e) Ragazze, dove sono le **vostre** amiche?

f) La **nostra** cultura è molto interessante perché siamo un popolo antico.

g) Bambini, chi sono i **vostri** genitori?

h) La **nostra** fortuna è stata che vi abbiamo incontrati.

i) Mario e Susanna hanno cambiato macchina, la **loro** era molto vecchia.

j) Devo chiamare Giulia e dirle che la **sua** macchina è pronta.

3.12 Presente indicativo

3.12.1 Fill in the gaps with the correct form of the 1st person singular of the presente indicativo of verbs in brackets:

Ciao, 1. **mi chiamo** Thomas e 2. **sono** di Cracovia, ma 3. **abito** a Roma da qualche mese. Per adesso 4. **vivo** in albergo ma 5. **cerco** casa. Da un po' di tempo 6. **guardo** gli annunci online ma non 7. **trovo** nulla di interessante. Domani 8. **vado** in agenzia e 9. **spero** di trovare una persona che mi aiuti. 10. **ho** molta fiducia.

3.12.2 Fill in the gaps with the correct form of the 3rd person singular of the presente indicativo of verbs in brackets:

Lui 1. **si chiama** Thomas e 2. **è** di Cracovia, ma 3. **abita** a Roma da qualche mese. Per adesso 4. **vive** in albergo ma 5. **cerca** casa. Da un po' di tempo 6. **guarda** gli annunci online ma non 7. **trova** nulla di interessante. Domani 8. **va** in agenzia e 9. **spera** di trovare una persona che lo aiuti. 10. **ha** molta fiducia.

3.13 Past tenses

3.13.1 Fill in the gaps with the correct form of the passato prossimo or imperfetto of verbs in brackets:

Un pappagallo 1. **è scappato** di casa: 2. **è successo** qualche giorno fa a Milano. I proprietari 3. **erano** molto tristi ma 4. **hanno raccontato** la storia del pappagallo ai giornali. 5. **Si chiamava** Ugo e per loro 6. **era** come un figlio. Lo 7. **lasciavano** sempre libero in casa, ma un giorno il vento 8. **ha aperto** la finestra e lui 9. **è volato** via. Fortunatamente lo 10. **hanno ritrovato** pochi giorni dopo grazie all'aiuto di molti cittadini.

3.14 Combined personal pronouns

3.14.1 Fill in the gaps with the correct combined personal pronoun:

a) Porto alla nonna la torta - **Gliela** porto.

I am taking it to her.

b) Ci scrivi il tuo indirizzo? - **Ce lo** scrivi?

Can you write it to us?

c) Per Natale regalo un viaggio a Mario - **Glielo** regalo per Natale.

I am giving it to her for Christmas.

d) Chi vi presta la macchina per il viaggio? - Chi **ve la** presta?

Who is lending it to you?

e) Hanno scritto un messaggio ai loro amici - **Gliel'** hanno scritto.

They have written it to them.

f) Mi spieghi l'esercizio che non l'ho capito? - **Me lo** spieghi che non l'ho capito?

Could you explain it to me?

g) Avete chiesto a Paola se voleva venire anche lei? - **Glielo** avete chiesto?

Did you ask her about it?

h) Ti hanno già consegnato il pacco? - **Te lo** hanno già consegnato?

Have they already delivered it to you?

i) Avete comprato i cioccolatini al nonno? - **Glieli** avete comprati?

Have you bought them for him?

j) Ho regalato una collana alla mia fidanzata - **Gliel'**ho regalata.

I have given it to her

Section 4 – Dialogues

In this section, you will see the practical use of all the grammar seen in sections 1 and 2.

4.1 Basic greetings

"Ciao" is internationally known and used, but in many countries, it is used only to greet when it is time to go. In Italian, "ciao" represents the informal greeting, both when you meet a person and when you leave. Going away, you can also say, "ci vediamo" - see you. If you want to be formal when you meet a person, you may greet him or her using "salve", which is generic and can be used during any moment of the day. Of course, you can always say "buongiorno", if it is morning, and "buonasera" for the evening, which starts at sunset. Still being formal and wanting to greet someone when going away, you may use "arrivederci" or "buonanotte" after dinner. Please consider that "buongiorno" and "buonanotte" can also be used in informal contexts. Furthermore, there are the expressions "buona giornata" and "buona serata", which mean "have a good day" and "have a good evening/night".

4.2 The time

This is not a difficult topic if you consider that, in Italian, you tell the hour beforehand and the minutes right afterward. See the main translations: "o'clock" will be "in punto", but it is also possible to leave it out; "half" is "mezzo" and "quarter" is "un quarto". Now consider that when English uses "past" (to say minutes passed after the hour), Italian uses "e" (to add passed minutes to the hour); when English uses "to" (to say minutes left to the next hour), Italian uses "meno" (to indicate minutes that are left to the hour). English always uses "is", while Italian uses "sono"—hours are plural except "one", which uses "è" because it is the only one to be singular. Here are some examples:

It's four o'clock - sono le quattro (in punto)

It's quarter past four - sono le quattro e un quarto

It's half past four - sono le quattro e mezzo

It's quarter to five - sono le cinque meno un quarto

It's five to five - sono le cinque meno cinque

As you can see, in Italian, you tell the hour beforehand and the minutes that are passed or left right afterward.

Moreover, "midnight" corresponds to "mezzanotte" and "midday" to "mezzogiorno", and they are used with "è". For example: "è mezzanotte".

4.3 Introducing yourself

4.3.1 Informal - informale

a. Ciao! Io mi chiamo Maria, tu come ti chiami?

Hi! My name is Maria, what's your name?

b. Ciao! Mi chiamo Paul, molto piacere

Hi! My name is Paul, nice to meet you.

a. Piacere mio! Di dove sei?

Nice to meet you too! Where are you from?

b. Sono dell'Inghilterra ma vivo a Roma da tre anni. Studio medicina all'università. Tu?

I'm from England, but I've been living in Rome for three years. I study medicine at university. You?

a. Sono italiana, vengo da Napoli ma anch'io vivo a Roma e lavoro in una banca. Quanti anni hai? Io ne ho 26.

I'm Italian, I come from Naples, but I live in Rome just like you and work in a bank. How old are you? I'm 26.

b. Ho 23 anni ma tra poco ne compio 24.

I'm 23, but I'm turning 24 soon.

<u>4.3.2. Formal - formale</u>

a. Buongiono, Signora, come posso aiutarla?

Good morning, Madame, how can I help you?

b. Buongiorno, dovrei iscrivermi al corso di yoga.

Good morning, I would like to join the yoga class.

a. Bene, come si chiama?

Good, what's your name?

b. Mi chiamo Sonia.

My name is Sonia.

a. Qual è il suo cognome?

What's your last name?

b. Rossi.

a. Quando è nata? (data di nascita)

When were you born? (date of birth)

b. Sono nata il 4 agosto del 1983 a Milano.

I was born on August 4th, 1983, in Milan.

a. Dove vive?

Where do you live?

b. Vivo qui a Milano.

I live here in Milan.

a. Qual è il suo indirizzo?

What's your address?

b. Via Bragazzi 20

a. Che lavoro fa?

What's your job?

b. Sono un'insegnante.

I'm a teacher.

a. Mi lascia il suo numero di cellulare e un indirizzo email?

Could you give me your phone number and email address?

b. Certamente! Il mio numero di cellulare è 36298465 e il mio indirizzo email è s.rossi@xmail.com (esse punto rossi chiocciola xmail punto com)

Sure! My phone number is 36298465 and my email address is s.rossi@xmail.com (es dot rossi at xmail dot com)

a. Perfetto, ora firmi qui per cortesia.

Perfect, now sign here, please.

b. Ecco.

Here you are.

a. Arrivederci signora Rossi.

Bye-bye.

b. Arrivederci.

Bye-bye.

4.3.3 Questions

1. Di dov'è Paul?

Where is Paul from?

2. Di dov'è Maria?
Where is Maria from?

3. Che cosa studia Paul?
What does Paul study?

4. Dove vivono Paul e Maria?
Where do Paul and Maria live?

5. Che lavoro fa Maria?
What is Maria's job?

6. Quanti anni ha Paul?
How old is Paul?

7. Quando è nata la signora Sonia?
When was Mrs. Sonia born?

8. Che lavoro fa la signora Sonia?
What is Mrs. Sonia's job?

9. Come si chiama la signora Sonia di cognome?
What is Mrs. Sonia's surname?

10. Dove vive la signora Sonia?
Where does Mrs. Sonia live?

4.3.4 Answer keys

1. Dell'Inghilterra.
From England.

2. Di Napoli.
From Naples.

3. Medicina.
Medicine.

4. A Roma.
In Rome.

5. Lavora in banca.

She works in a bank.

6. 23.

7. Il 4 agosto del 1983.

On August 4th, 1983.

8. L'insegnante.

The teacher.

9. Rossi

10. A Milano.

In Milan.

4.3.5 Informal – informale: meeting people in a club – conoscere persone in un locale

a. Nicola; b. Alessandro; c. Martina; d. Laura; e. Barman - barista

b. Che bel locale, non c'ero mai stato prima, è nuovo?

What a nice club? I have never been here before, is it new?

a. Sì, lo hanno aperto circa due mesi fa. Ci sono venuto per la prima volta la settimana scorsa con mio fratello e alcuni suoi amici. Ci siamo divertiti molto.

Yes, it is. It opened about two months ago. I first came here last week with my brother and some friends of his. We had a lot of fun.

b. Prendiamo qualcosa da bere?

Shall we get a drink?

a. Certo!

Sure!

e. Buonasera, ragazzi, che cosa vi preparo?

Goodnight, guys, what can I prepare for you?

a. Per me un vodka – tonic

For me a vodka-tonic

b. Anche per me grazie.

I'll go with the same one, thanks.

e. Ecco qui, sono 14 euro.

Here you are, it is 14 euros.

b. Lascia, offro io!

No, I got it!

a. Grazie, il prossimo giro è mio!

Thank you, next round is on me!

b. Guarda quelle due ragazze laggiù, quelle vicino alla porta; non sono carine?

Look at those girls over there, the ones near the door; aren't they nice?

a. Ah, Alessandro si è messo subito al lavoro! Andiamo a conoscerle!

Ah, Alessandro immediately begun to work! Let's go and meet them!

b. Naturalmente, mi sono lasciato ormai da un mese ed è ora di conoscere nuove ragazze!

Of course, I broke up almost one month ago and it is time to meet new girls!

a. Ciao, ragazze, possiamo sederci con voi al vostro tavolo?

Hi, girls, can we take a seat with you at your table?

d. Va bene; c'è abbastanza spazio per tutti.

That's ok; there is enough space for everyone.

b. Piacere, mi chiamo Alessandro e lui è Nicola. Voi?

My name is Alessandro, nice to meet you. He is Nicola, and you?

d. Io mi chiamo Laura e questa è mia cugina, Martina.

My name is Laura and this is my cousin, Martina.

a. Venite spesso qui?

Do you often come here?

c. Da quando ha aperto siamo venute 2 volte; è un bel locale, e la musica è molto bella.

Since it has opened, we came here twice; it is a nice club, and the music is very good.

b. Hai ragione; è la prima volta che vengo ma ci tornerò sicuramente. Possiamo offrirvi qualcosa da bere?

You're right; this is the first time I come here, but I will definitely come back. Can we offer you something to drink?

c. Per me, no, grazie. Non bevo.

For me, no, thanks. I don't drink.

d. Per me, si, grazie.

For me, yes, please.

b. Che cosa ti posso prendere?

What can I get for you?

d. Un vodka-tonic.

A vodka-tonic.

b. Lo stesso che stiamo bevendo noi! Abbiamo già una cosa in comune...

The same drink we are having! We've already something in common...

[Alessando e Laura vanno a prendere da bere e tornano]

[Alessando and Laura go to order the drink and come back]

a. Martina mi stava raccontando che avere un negozio di vestiti in centro.

Martina was telling me you have a clothing shop downtown.

d. Sì, lo abbiamo aperto tre anni fa. Voi cosa fate, ragazzi?

Yes, we opened it three years ago. What do you do, guys?

a. Io sono avvocato, lavoro in uno studio legale che si occupa di cause civili.

I am an attorney; I work in a law firm, which deals with civil cases.

b. Io sono architetto, e lavoro come libero professionista e ho il mio ufficio a casa.

I am an architect, and I work freelance and have got my own office at home.

a. Basta con le domande; andiamo a ballare!

Enough with questions; let's go dancing!

b.c. e d. Andiamo!

Let's go!

4.3.5.1 Questions

1. Alessandro e Nicola sono mai stati in questo locale?

Have Alessandro and Nicola ever been to this club?

2. Che cosa prenodono da bere?

What do they drink?

3. Chi paga?

Who pays?

4. Che cosa chiede Nicola alle ragazze per conoscerle?

What does Nicola ask the girls (in order) to get to know them?

5. È la prima volta che Martina e Laura vanno in questo locale?

Is it the first time Martina and Laura go to this club?

6. Che cosa prendono Martina e Laura da bere?

What do Martina and Laura get to drink?

7. Con chi va Laura a prendere da bere?

Who does Laura go to get a drink with?

8. Cosa stava raccontando Martina a Nicola mentre gli altri erano a prendere da bere?

What was Martina telling Nicola while the others were getting drinks?

9. Che lavoro fanno Alessandro e Nicola, lavorano insieme?

What is Alessandro and Nicola's job? Do they work together?

10. Dove vanno insieme dopo essersi conosciuti?

Where do they go together after they had met?

4.3.5.2 Answer keys

1. Per Alessandro è la prima volta; Nicola invece c'è stato la settimana prima con suo fratello e alcuni suoi amici.

For Alessandro, it is the first time; while Nicola has been there the previous week with his brother and some friends of his.

2. Prendono due vodka-tonic.

They get two vodka-tonic.

3. Paga Alessandro; Nicola pagherà il giro dopo.

Alessandro pays; Nicola will pay the next round.

4. Gli chiede se possono sedersi con loro al loro tavolo.

He asks them if they can take a seat with them at their table.

5. No, è la seconda volta che ci vanno da quando ha aperto.

No, it is not. It is the second time they go there since it opened.

6. Laura prende un vodka-tonic; Martina niente perché non beve.

Laura gets a vodka-tonic; Martina nothing because she does not drink.

7. Con Alessandro.

With Alessandro.

8. Martina gli stava raccontando che Laura e lei hanno un negozio di vestiti in centro.

Martina was telling him that she and Laura have a clothing shop downtown.

9. Alessandro è un architetto e Nicola un avvocato. Non lavorano insieme perché Nicola lavora in uno studio legale e Alessandro è un libero professionista e ha il suo ufficio a casa.

Alessandro is an architect and Nicola is an attorney. They do not work together because Nicola works in a law office, and Alessandro is a freelancer and has got his own office at home.

10. Dopo essersi conosciuti vanno a ballare.

After they had met, they go dancing.

4.4 Buying and ordering

4.4.1 In a shop - in un negozio

a. Shop assistant - commesso; b. client - cliente

a. Buongiorno, posso aiutarla?

Good morning, can I help you?

b. Buongiorno, si. Vorrei provarmi quei pantaloni blu che sono in vetrina.

Good morning, yes. I would like to try on those blue trousers in the shop window.

a. Certo, che taglia le serve?

Sure, what size do you need?

b. Una small.

A small.

[il cliente entra nel camerino]

[the client goes into the fitting room]

a. Come le vanno?

How do they suit you?

b. Mi sembra bene, però vorrei provare anche la taglia più grande.

I think well, but I would like to try on also the bigger size.

a. Gliela prendo subito.

I'll take it immediately.

[il cliente entra nel camerino]

[the client goes into the fitting room]

b. Questi mi vanno decisamente meglio; è la mia taglia.

These suit me much better; it's my size.

a. Vuole vedere una camicia da abbinare al pantalone?

Would you like to see a shirt to match with the trousers?

b. No grazie, va bene così. Quanto costano?

No thanks, it's ok. How much do they cost?

a. Costano 120 euro. Paga in contanti, bancomat, o carta di credito?

They cost 120 euros. Do you pay by cash, debit, or credit card?

b. Carta di credito.

Credit card.

a. Posso avere un documento d'identità, per favore?

Could you give me an ID, please?

b. Certo, eccolo.

Sure, here you are.

a. Perfetto. Questo è il suo scontrino e questo il suo sacchetto. Arrivederci.

Perfect. Here is your receipt and your bag. Bye-bye.

b. Arrivederci.

Bye-bye.

4.4.1.1 Questions

1. Che cosa vuole provare il cliente?

What does the client want to try on?

2. Che taglia compra alla fine?

What size does he finally buy?

3. Che cosa la commessa gli propone da abbinare?

What does the shop assistant propose to match them with?

4. Quanto costano i pantaloni?

How much do the trousers cost?

5. Come paga il cliente?

How does the client pay?

4.4.1.2 Answer keys

1. Un paio di pantaloni blu.

A pair of blue trousers.

2. Una medium.

A medium.

3. Una camicia.

A shirt.

4. 120 euro.

120 euros.

5. Con carta di credito.

With credit card.

4.4.2. Buying online - comprare online

a. Ciao, Elena, come stai?

Hi, Elena, how are you?

b. Ciao, Sonia! Bene, grazie. Tu?

Hi, Sonia! Fine, thanks. You?

a. Bene. Hai visto i saldi sul sito magia.com?

I'm good. Have you seen the sales on the website magia.com?

b. Non ancora. Hai fatto buoni affari?

Not yet. Have you made good deals?

a. Sì. Ho comprato un paio di scarpe con il tacco e una borsa di pelle nera al 50% di sconto. Nel carrello ho anche un paio di jeans ma c'è stato un problema con il pagamento, non mi fa procedere all'acquisto. È molto strano perché compro spesso su questo sito e il mio account non ha mai avuto problemi.

Yes. I bought a pair of heels and a black leather bag purse with 50% discount. In the cart, I also have a pair of jeans, but there's a problem with the paying process - I can't proceed with the purchase. It's very strange, as I often buy items on this website and my account has never had problems.

b. Hai provato a ricaricare la pagina?

Have you tried to refresh the page?

a. Si, ma non è successo nulla. Stasera riprovo e se non funziona contatterò il servizio clienti. Non voglio perdere quei jeans e non voglio pagare due spedizioni.

Yes, but nothing happened. Tonight, I'm trying again, and if it doesn't work, I'll contact the customer service.

b. Non ti preoccupare, vedrai che stasera ci riesci. Una volta è capitato anche a me. Volevo prenotare un volo Roma-Parigi ma il sito non caricava la pagina del pagamento. Ci ho provato il giorno dopo e ha funzionato.

Don't worry. You'll see - you'll sort it out tonight. Once it happened to me too. I wanted to book a Rome-Paris flight, but the website didn't load the payment page.

a. Bene, ti farò sapere come è andata a finire.

Good, I'll let you know how it goes.

4.4.2.1 Questions

1. Dove ha fatto acquisti Sonia?

Where has Sonia shopped?

2. Che cosa ha comprato?

What has she bought?

3. Che problema ha avuto Sonia con i Jeans?

What problem did she have with jeans?

4. Che cosa le suggerisce di fare Elena?

What does Elena suggest she do?

5. Quando Elena ha avuto un problema simile a quello di Sonia?

Did Elena have a similar problem to Sonia's one and when?

4.4.2.2 Answer keys

1. Su magia.com

On magia.com.

2. Un paio di pantaloni e una borsa di pelle.

A pair of trousers and a leather bag.

3. Il sito non le caricava la pagina per il pagamento.

The website didn't upload the payment page.

4. Di ricaricare la pagina.

To refresh the page.

5. Quando voleva prenotare un volo Roma-Parigi.

When she wanted to book a Rome-Paris flight.

4.5 At work

4.5.1 Getting ready for a meeting – preparandosi per una riunione.

a. Buongiorno, Giulia!

Good morning, Giulia!

b. Buongiorno, Signor Carli!

Good morning, Mr. Carli!

a. Oggi abbiamo molto lavoro da fare e sono arrivato in ritardo perché c'era molto traffico.

Today, we have a lot of work to do and I arrived late because there was a lot of traffic.

b. Lo so; ho già stampato tutta la documentazione per la riunione di oggi, anche l'ordine del giorno.

I know; I've already printed all documentation of the meeting today, the agenda too.

a. Brava, ottimo lavoro! A che ora arriva il consiglio?

Good, good job! What time does the board arrive?

b. Tra un'ora, alle 10.

In one hour, at 10 o'clock.

a. Bene, abbiamo ancora tempo. Allora, apri la cartella "fatture" sul mio computer e stampa tutte quelle dell'ultimo mese. Poi controlla la tua email e scarica tutti i file che ti ho inviato ieri sera e stampali.

Well, we still have time. So, open the folder "invoices" on my laptop and download all of the last month. Then check your email and download all files I sent you yesterday and print them.

b. Va bene, lo faccio subito. Ecco qui!

Ok, I'll do it right now. Here you are!

a. Queste sono le indicazioni per il mese, per i venditori e la dirigenza. Dove sono i curricula da analizzare per i posti vacanti?

These are indications for the month, for the salespeople and the management. Where are the CVs that have to be analyzed for open positions?

b. Li ha la responsabile delle risorse umane; sono già selezionati per i colloqui.

The HR has them; they are already selected for interviews.

a. Ho preparato il piano per gli incentivi e compensi per il prossimo semestre e anche per gli stipendi. Ho qualche appuntamento dopo?

I've also prepared the planning for bonuses and commissions for next semester and also for wages. Do I have any appointments after?

b. No, le ho cancellato tutti gli appuntamenti della giornata. Dovrebbe solo fare una chiamata al Signor Bassi per chiudere l'accordo della settimana scorsa.

No, you haven't. I've cleared your schedule for the day. You may only make a call to Mr. Bassi to close last week's agreement.

a. Molto bene, allora direi che abbiamo tutto pronto. Sei un'ottima segretaria.

Very well, so I'd say we have everything ready. You're a perfect secretary.

b. La ringrazio Signor Carli, lei è un capo eccezionale.

Thank you, Mr. Carli, you're an excellent boss.

4.5.2 Questions

1. Perché il Signor Carli è arrivato tardi al lavoro?

Why did Mr. Carli arrive late at work?

2. Che cosa ha già stampato Giulia?

What has Giulia already printed?

3. A che ora arriva il consiglio?

What time does the board arrive?

4. Dove sono i file che Giulia deve stampare dal computer?

Where are the files Giulia has to print from the computer?

5. Che altro deve stampare Giulia?

What else does Giulia have to print?

6. Che cosa ha preparato il Signor Carli per i venditori e la dirigenza?

What did Mr. Carli prepare for salespersons and the management?

7. Chi ha i curricula per le posizioni aperte?

Who has the CVs for the open positions?

8. Che cosa ha già preparato il Signor Carli per il semestre successivo?

What has Mr. Carli already prepared for the following semester?

9. Quali altri impegni ha il Signor Carli per la giornata?

What other appointments does Mr. Carli have for the day?

10. Perché Giulia ringrazia il Signor Carli?

Why did Giulia thank Mr. Carli?

4.5.3 Answer keys

1. Perché c'era molto traffico.

Because there was a lot of traffic.

2. La documentazione per il meeting e l'ordine del giorno.

The documentation for the meeting and the agenda.

3. Alle dieci.

At ten o'clock.

4. Nella cartella "fatture".

In the "invoices" folder.

5. I file che il Signor Carli le ha mandato la sera prima via email.

Files Mr. Carli sent her the night before.

6. Le indicazioni del mese.

Instructions for the month.

7. La responsabile delle risorse umane.

The HR head.

8. Gli incentivi, i compensi, e gli stipendi.

Bonuses, commissions, and wages.

9. Deve solo chiamare il Signor Bassi per chiudere l'accordo della settimana prima.

He only has to call Mr. Bassi to close the agreement of the week before.

10. Perché le ha detto che è un'ottima segretaria.

Because he told her she is a great secretary.

4.6 At school

4.6.1 First day at the college - primo giorno all'università

a./b. students; c. professor

a. Scusami, sai dov'è la lezione del Professor Fossa? È il mio primo giorno all'università e devo ancora orientarmi. Ci sono molte aule e non so ancora dove sono.

Excuse me, do you know where Professor Fossa's lesson is? It's my first day at college, and I still have to find my bearings. There are many classrooms, and I don't know where they are yet.

b. Certo! Capisco, i primi giorni sono sempre i più difficili, ma vedrai che in meno di una settimana saprai orientarti alla perfezione. Comunque, io sto andando proprio alla sua lezione, quindi seguimi.

Sure! I know, first days are always the most difficult, but you will see - in less than one week, you will be able to orient yourself perfectly. Anyway, I'm going exactly to his class, so follow me.

a. Perfetto, sono stato proprio fortunato. Comunque io mi chiamo Pietro.

Perfect, I've been very lucky. I'm Pietro by the way.

b. Piacere. Io mi chiamo Luca. Di dove sei?

Nice to meet you. I'm Luca. Where are you from?

a. Sono di Rimini e tu?

I'm from Rimini, and you?

b. Anch'io! Come è possibile che non ci siamo mai visti prima? Rimini è una città piccola.

Me too! How is it possible that you have never met before? Rimini is a small town.

a. In effetti è incredibile. Quanti anni hai?

It is indeed unbelievable. How old are you?

b. Ho 20 anni. Tu?

I'm 20, you?

a. Io ho 19 anni. Quindi abbiamo più o meno la stessa età. Che scuola hai frequentato?

I'm 19. So, we are the same age, more or less. Which school did you attend?

b. Mi sono diplomato all'istituto tecnico, tu?

I graduated at the technical institute, you?

a. Anch'io, ma a quello di Cattolica, perché prima vivevo lì con la mia famiglia. Ci siamo trasferiti quando ero al secondo anno e non volevo cambiare scuola.

Me too, but in Cattolica, because I used to live there with my family. We moved when I was in my second year, and I didn't want to change school.

b. Facevi un lungo viaggio tutte le mattine!

You took a long drive every morning!

a. Si, infatti mi svegliavo molto presto. In autobus ci voleva un'ora, ma quando mi portava mio padre in macchina potevo alzarmi un pochino dopo.

Yes, I did. I used to wake up early. It took one hour by bus, but when my father took me by car, I could wake up a bit later.

b. Ok, siamo arrivati! Questa è l'aula del Professor Fossa. È molto bravo ma anche molto esigente, infatti lo scorso anno non ho passato l'esame e ora deve rifrequentare le lezioni.

Ok, we've arrived! This is Professor Fossa's classroom. He is very good but very demanding too, in fact I didn't pass the exam last year and now I have to attend his lessons again.

c. Buongiorno, a tutti! Sono il Professor Fossa and e questo è il corso di Meccatronica. Alcuni di voi sono nuovi studenti, quindi benvenuti. Altri sono vecchi studenti e quindi, ben tornati. Come i vostri compagni, quelli che non hanno passato l'esame lo scorso anno, posso dirvi che sono molto esigente, ma se frequentate le lezioni e prendete appunti sono sicuro che passerete l'esame senza alcun problema. Per qualsiasi domanda, vi prego di venirmi a trovare nel mio ufficio. Sarò lieto di rispondere ai vostri quesiti. Il mio orario di ricevimento è lunedì e venerdì dalle 9 del mattino alle 13; mercoledì e giovedì dalle 2 alle 5 del pomeriggio. Se avete qualche problema a venire in questi giorni e orari, per favore scrivetemi una email e prenderemo un appuntamento.

Good morning, everyone! I'm Professor Fossa, and this is the Mechatronics course. Some of you are new students, so welcome. Others are old students, and so, welcome back. As your classmates, those who didn't pass the exam last year, can tell you, I'm very demanding, but if you attend classes and take note, I'm sure you will pass the exam without any kind of problems. For any questions, please come to visit me in my office. I'll be glad to answer your queries. My office hours are Monday and Friday from 9 am to 1 pm; Wednesday and Thursday from 2 pm to 5 pm. If you have any difficulties to come on these days and times, please write me an email, and we will set up an appointment.

a. Non sembra così cattivo come dici!

He doesn't seem to be as bad as you said!

b. Fidati, lo vedrai all'esame!

Trust me, you will see at the exam!

c. Ok, per oggi è tutto. Ci vediamo la prossima settimana.

Ok, that's all for today. See you next week.

b. Vado in biblioteca per mettere in ordine gli appunti, vieni con me?

I'm going to the library to order notes, are you coming with me?

a. Si, perché no! Così imparo anche dove si trova.

Yes, why not! So I also learn where it is.

b. Perfetto! Ti mostro anche la mensa; è di strada.

Perfect! I'll show you the canteen too; it's on the way.

4.6.2 Questions

1. Quale aula sta cercando Pietro?

What classroom is Pietro looking for?

2. Da dove viene Luca?

Where is Luca from?

3. Quale scuola ha frequentato? E Pietro?

Which school did he attend? And Pietro?

4. Perchè Pietro ha frequentato la scuola a Cattolica?

Why did Pietro attend the school in Cattolica?

5. Come andava a scuola Pietro?

How did Pietro used to go to school?

6. Perché Luca frequenta di nuovo le lezioni del Professor Fossa?

Why is Luca attending Professor Fossa's classes again?

7. Quali sono i consigli del Professor Fossa per passare l'esame?

What are Professor Fossa's tips to pass the exam?

8. Quali sono i giorni di ricevimento del Professor Fossa?

What is Professor Fossa's office time?

9. Dove vanno Pietro e Luca dopo la lezione?

Where are Pietro and Luca going after the class?

10. Che cosa Luca mostrerà a Pietro?

What is Luca going to show Pietro?

4.6.3 Answer keys

1. Pietro sta cercando l'aula del Professor Fossa.

Pietro is looking for Professor Fossa's classroom.

2. Luca viene da Rimini.

Luca comes from Rimini.

3. Tutti e due hanno frequentato l'istituto tecnico.

They both attended the technical institute.

4. Perché viveva lì con la sua famiglia e quando si sono trasferiti Pietro non voleva cambiare scuola.

Because they lived there with his family and when they moved, Pietro didn't want to change school.

5. In autobus o in macchina con suo padre.

By bus or by car with his father.

6. Perché non ha passato l'esame l'anno precedente.

Because he didn't pass the exam the previous year.

7. Frequentare le lezioni e prendere appunti.

To attend classes and take notes.

8. Lunedì, mercoledì, giovedì, e venerdì.

Monday, Wednesday, Thursday, and Friday.

9. In biblioteca.

At the library.

10. La mensa.

The canteen.

4.7 Traveling

4.7.1 At the station - alla stazione

a. traveler b. station worker

a. Buonasera, vorrei un'informazione.

Good evening, I would like information.

b. Buonasera a lei, mi dica pure.

Good evening to you, please tell me.

a. Vorrei sapere quando parte il prossimo treno per Roma; ho finito di lavorare tardi, e ho perso quello delle 16:40.

I would like to know when the next train to Rome is leaving; I finished work late, and I missed the 16:40 one.

b. Ce n'è uno alle 17:00 e un altro alle 17:30. Quello delle 17:00 arriva alle 18:30 perché è un treno regionale e fa alcune fermate intermedie, e costa 15 euro. Quello delle 17:30 invece è un diretto; anche quello arriva alle 18 e costa 28 euro.

There is one at 17:00 and another at 17:30. The one at 17:00 arrives at 18:30 because it is a regional train and has some extra stops, it costs 15 euros. The one at 17:30 is direct; it also arrives at 18:30 and costs 28 euros.

a. Allora prenderò quello delle 17:00, così non aspetto troppo tempo in stazione. Dove posso comprare i biglietti?

So, I will take the 17:00 one, so I'm not waiting too much in the station. Where can I buy tickets?

b. In biglietteria, ma se c'è coda le conviene andare alla biglietteria automatica.

At the ticket office, if there is a line, it is better for you to go to the ticket machine.

a. E posso pagare con carta di credito anche alla biglietteria automatica?

And can I pay by credit card at the ticket machine too?

b. Certamente. Accetta contanti, bancomat, e carta di credito.

Sure. It accepts cash, debit, and credit cards.

a. Va bene, grazie. Un'ultima cosa: da quale binario parte il treno?

Ok, thanks. One last thing: Which platform does the train leave from?

b. Dal binario 8. Per fare prima usi il sottopassaggio.

From platform 8. To be faster, use the underpass.

a. Perfetto, grazie.

Perfect, thank you.

4.7.1.1 Questions

1. Che treno ha perso il viaggiatore?

What train does the traveler lose?

2. Perché ha perso il treno?

Why did he lose the train?

3. Quali treni può prendere dopo?

Which trains can he take after?

4. Quale treno arriva prima? Perché?

Which train does arrive before? Why?

5. Quale treno costa meno?

Which train does cost less?

6. Quale decide di prendere il viaggiatore? Perché?

Which does the traveler decide to take? Why?

7. Dove può comprare i biglietti?

Where can he buy tickets?

8. Può pagare in contanti alla biglietteria automatica?

Can he pay by cash at the ticket machine?

9. Da che binario parte il treno?

Which platform does the train leave from?

10. Come può raggiungere quel binario?

How can he reach the platform?

4.7.1.2 Answer keys

1. Quello delle 16:40.

The 16:40 one.

2. Perché ha finito di lavorare tardi.

Because he finished work late.

3. Può prendere quello delle 17:00 e quello delle 17:30

He can take the 17:00 and 17:30 ones.

4. Arrivano tutti e due alle 18:30 perché quello delle 17:30 è un treno diretto e non ha fermate intermedie, mentre quello delle 17:00 è un treno regionale e ha fermate intermedie.

They both arrive at 18:30 because the 17:30 is a direct train and doesn't do extra stops, while the 17:00 is a regional train and has extra stops.

5. Quello regionale.

The regional one.

6. Quello regionale così non deve aspettare troppo in stazione.

The regional one so he does not have to wait too much in the station.

7. Sia in biglietteria che alla biglietteria automatica.

Both at the ticket office and at the ticket machine.

8. No, può pagare anche con bancomat o carta di credito.

No, he can also pay with debit or credit cards.

9. Dal binario 8.

From platform 8.

10. Con il sottopassaggio.

By the underpass.

4.7.2 At the airport – all'aeroporto

a./b. travelers; c. airline company employee

a. Bene, siamo arrivati. Ora, questo è il terminal degli arrivi e noi dobbiamo andare a quello delle partenze dei voli internazionali che è là.

Well, we've arrived. Further up is the arrivals terminal and we have to go to the international departures terminal that is there.

b. Ok, allora scarichiamo le valigie.

Ok, so let's unload our suitcases.

[al check-in]

[at the check-in]

c. Buongiorno! Prego, biglietti, passaporto, e mettete le valigie sulla bilancia.

Good morning, tickets, passports, and put your suitcases on the scale, please.

a. Ecco qui, Giulia, dammi il tuo.

Here you are. Giulia, give yours.

c. Avete solo queste due? Bagagli a mano?

Do you have only these two? Any hand luggage?

a. Si, solo queste. Come bagaglio a mano abbiamo solo questo zaino.

Yes, only these ones. As hand luggage, we have only this backpack.

c. Bene, ci metta questa etichetta. Allora, queste sono le vostre carte d'imbarco, l'orario di apertura del gate è alle 10:20. Chiude alle 10:50. Ricordate che non sono ammessi liquidi sopra i 100 ml e ricordatevi di presentare la carta d'imbarco all'addetto alla sicurezza prima dei controlli. Ricordate inoltre di guardare i monitor circa 10 minuti prima dell'inizio dell'imbarco per conoscere il numero del gate.

Fine, so put this tag on. So, these are your boarding cards, gate opens at 10:20 and closes at 10:50. Remember that liquids over 100 ml are not allowed and remember to show the boarding card to the safety officer before the security control area. Remember also to look at screens about 10 minutes before boarding to check the gate number.

a. Tutto chiaro, grazie.

All clear, thanks.

b. Bene, abbiamo ancora un po' di tempo, così possiamo fare un giro per i negozi e mangiare qualcosa prima di imbarcarci.

Well, we still have some time, so we can take a walk around the shops and have something to eat before boarding.

a. Non siamo ancora partite e già vuoi comprare qualcosa? Per il ritorno dovremmo comprare una nuova valigia!

We haven't left yet and you already want to buy something? For the return, we should buy a new suitcase!

b. Hai ragione; aspetterò il ritorno per fare acquisti in aeroporto. Prendiamoci un caffè!

You're right; I will wait for the return to shop in the airport. Let's have a coffee!

a. Bell'idea e sicuramente più economica!

Good idea and definitely cheaper!

4.7.2.1 Questions

1. A quale terminal devono recarsi i viaggiatori?

Which terminal should the travelers go to?

2. Quanti bagagli hanno i viaggiatori?

How many suitcases do the travelers have?

3. Quanti bagagli a mano hanno i viaggiatori?

How many hand luggage do the travelers have?

4. Che cosa dà l'impiegato della compagnia aerea ai viaggiatori da mettere sul bagaglio a mano?

What does the airline employee give to the travelers to put on the hand luggage?

5. A che ora inizia l'imbarco? A che ora chiude il gate?

What time does the boarding start? What time does the gate close?

6. Che cosa devono mostrare i viaggiatori all'addetto alla sicurezza?

What do the travelers have to show to the safety officer?

7. Che cosa devono controllare i viaggiatori sul monitor 10 minuti prima dell'apertura del gate?

What do the travelers have to check on screens 10 minutes before the gate opens?

8. Che cosa vuole fare Giulia prima di imbarcarsi?

What does Giulia want to do before boarding?

9. Quando comprerà qualcosa in aeroporto?

When will she buy something in the airport?

10. Perché alla fine Giulia propone di prendere un caffè?

Why does Giulia propose to have a coffee?

4.7.2.2 Answer keys

1. Al terminal delle partenze internazionali.

At the international departure terminal.

2. Ne hanno due.

They have two.

3. Ne hanno uno.

They have one.

4. Un'etichetta.

A tag.

5. L'imbarco inizia alle 10:20 e chiude alle 10:50.

Boarding starts at 10:20 and closes at 10:50.

6. Il loro passaporto.

Their passports.

7. Il numero del gate.

The gate number.

8. Vuole comprare qualcosa.

She wants to buy something.

9. Perché la sua amica le dice che altrimenti dovrebbero comprare una valigia più grande per il ritorno.

Because her friend tells her they should buy another bigger suitcase for the return.

10. Al ritorno.

On the return.

4.7.3 Booking a hotel – prenotare un albergo

a. customer; b. receptionist

b. Albergo Serena buongiorno, sono Sara. Come posso aiutarla?

Hotel Serena good morning, Sara speaking. How can I help you?

a. Buongiorno, vorrei prenotare una stanza per la settimana dal 15 al 22 luglio.

Good morning, I would like to book a room for the week from 15th to 22nd July.

b. Una camera singola o doppia?

A single or a double room?

a. Una camera doppia, per cortesia.

A double room, please.

b. Mi faccia controllare. Per quella settimana abbiamo disponibile solo una camera vista mare.

Let me check. For that week, we have only a sea view room available.

a. E quanto costa?

And how much does it cost?

b. 90 euro al giorno con sola colazione inclusa.

90 euro per day with breakfast included.

a. C'è anche possibilità di scegliere la pensione completa?

Is there the opportunity to have full-board?

b. No, mi dispiace signora, al massimo potete scegliere la mezza pensione. Il nostro ristorante è aperto anche per cena, ma è solo alla carta.

No, there isn't, sorry. At most, you can have half-board. Our restaurant is open for dinner too but only a la carte.

a. Va bene, allora prenoterò la soluzione a mezza pensione. Quanto costa in più?

Ok, I will book the half-board solution. How much does it cost?

b. 20 euro al giorno. Consideri che deve anche aggiungere la tassa di soggiorno che è di 5 euro al giorno per persona.

20 euro per day. Consider that you have to add the local tax, which is 5 euro per day per person.

a. Va bene, voglio prenotare.

That's fine. I want to book.

b. Mi può fornire i suoi dati per cortesia?

Could you give me your personal information?

a. Certamente. Mi chiamo Manuela Fierro, nata il 03 marzo del 1976 a Bologna. Vivo a Bologna in via della Canonica numero 20.

Of course. My name is Manuela Fierro, born on March 3rd in 1976, in Bologna. I live in Bologna, via della Canonica number 20.

    b. Un recapito telefonico e un indirizzo email, per favore?

    A contact number and email, please?

    a. Il mio numero di cellulare è 3749921564 e il mio indirizzo email è m.fierro@xmail.com

    My cell phone number is 3749921564 and my email address is m.fierro@xmail.com.

    b. Perfetto. Ora le invio una email con i dati per il pagamento con carta di credito o bonifico.

    Perfect. I'm sending an email now with payment instructions by credit card or bank transfer.

    a. Devo pagare tutto l'importo?

    Do I have to pay the sum total?

    b. No, solo la caparra. Salderà qui da noi il giorno della partenza. Ha tempo fino a 3 giorni prima per cancellare la prenotazione e, in quel caso, il deposito le verrà rimborsato completamente.

    No, you don't. Only a down payment. You will pay the balance here on the departure day. You have until 3 days before to cancel your booking and, in this case, the down payment will be fully refunded.

    a. Va bene. Mi può dare un'ulteriore informazione?

    Ok. Could you give me further information?

    b. Certamente, mi dica.

    Sure, please tell me.

    a. Affittate auto all'hotel?

    Do you rent cars at the hotel?

    b. No, ma non le consiglio di affittare un'auto. Non ci sono molti parcheggi, e i pochi che ci sono costano molto. Qui accanto c'è un negozio che affitta biciclette o motorini che sono più comodi per visitare le spiagge e raggiungere i punti d'interesse turistico della zona.

No, we don't. But I do not suggest you to rent a car. There are not many parking areas, and those few cost a lot. Here, next to the hotel, there is a shop that rents bicycles and motor scooters, which are more comfortable to reach beaches and local touristic points of interest.

a. Perfetto, molto gentile. Grazie mille.

Perfect, very kind. Thank you so much.

b. Non c'è di che, e l'aspettiamo. Arrivederci.

You are welcome, and we are waiting for you. Bye-bye.

a. Arrivederci.

Bye-bye.

4.7.3.1 Questions

1. Perché la cliente chiama l'albergo Serena?

Why is the client calling Hotel Serena?

2. Che camera ha disponibile l'albergo per la settimana dal 15 al 22 luglio?

Which room does the hotel have available for the week from 15th to 22nd July?

3. Quando costa con colazione inclusa?

How much does it cost with breakfast included?

4. L'albergo offre l'opzione pensione completa?

Does the hotel offer the full-board option?

5. Quanto costa la tassa di soggiorno?

How much does the local tax cost?

6. Dove è nata la signora Fierro?

Where was Mrs. Fierro Born?

7. Come potrà pagare l'albergo?

How will she be able to pay the hotel?

8. Se cancella due giorni prima, l'albergo le rimborsa il deposito?

If she cancels two days before, will the hotel refund her the down payment?

9. Che cosa chiede infine la signora Fierro alla receptionist?

What does Mrs. Fierro ask the receptionist?

10. Che cosa consiglia di affittare la receptionist al posto della macchina? Perché?

What does the receptionist suggest to rent instead of the car? Why?

4.7.3.2 Answer keys

1. Perché vuole prenotare una camera doppia per una settimana a luglio.

Because she wants to book a double room for one week in July.

2. Una camera vista mare.

A sea view room.

3. 90 euro al giorno.

90 euros per day.

4. No, perché il ristorante offre la cena solo alla carta.

No, it doesn't. Because the restaurant offers only dinner a la carte.

5. 5 euro al giorno per persona.

5 euro per day per person.

6. A Bologna.

In Bologna.

7. Con carta di credito o con bonifico.

With credit card or bank transfer.

8. No, glielo rimborsano completamente se cancella almeno 3 giorni prima.

No, it won't. It will fully refund if she cancels it 3 days before.

9. Le chiede se l'albergo affitta delle macchine.

She asks her if the hotel rents cars.

10. Le consiglia di affittare una bicicletta o un motorino perché i parcheggi costano molto e la macchina è più scomoda.

She suggests she rent a bicycle or a motor scooter because parking costs a lot and the car is less comfortable.

4.7.4 At the restaurant – al ristorante

a./c. customer; b. waiter

a. Buonasera, ho prenotato un tavolo per 2 persone alle 9.

Good evening, I have booked a table for 2 people at 9 o'clock.

b. Buonasera, a che nome?

Good evening, what name?

a. Signora Petrelli.

Mrs. Petrelli.

b. Certamente, mi segua per cortesia. Mentre aspetta, le posso portare qualcosa da bere?

Sure, follow me, please. Could I bring you something to drink while waiting?

a. Si, grazie, una bottiglia di acqua frizzante, per favore.

Yes, please, a bottle of sparkling water, please.

b. Gliela porto subito.

I will bring it immediately.

[arriva l'altro cliente]

[the other client arrives]

a. Ciao, Mattia, ben arrivato. Come stai?

Hi, Mattia, welcome. How are you?

c. Ciao, Carla, bene e tu?

Hi. Carla, fine and you?

a. Bene, grazie. Ordiniamo; che ho molta fame?

Fine thanks. Let's order; I'm very hungry.

c. Certo. Che cosa fanno di buono qui?

Sure. What is good here?

a. Non lo so; è la prima volta che ci vengo. Chiediamo al cameriere.

I do not know; this is the first time I come here. Let's ask the waiter.

b. Siete pronti per ordinare?

Are you ready to order?

a. Si, che cosa ci consiglia?

Yes, what do you suggest?

b. I risotti sono eccezionali; sono le specialità della casa. Oggi fuori menù abbiamo il risotto di zucca con zucchine.

The risottos are excellent; they are the house specialties. Today, off menu, we have pumpkin risotto with zucchini.

a. Per me va bene questo.

This is ok for me.

c. Anche per me.

For me too.

b. Posso portarvi i nostri antipasti misti prima del risotto?

Can I bring you our mixed appetizers before the risotto?

c. Va bene, ma ci porti una sola porzione. Vorrei prendere un secondo dopo.

That's fine, but bring us only one serving. I would like to get a main course after.

b. D'accordo. Volete del vino?

All right. Would you like some wine?

c. Si, rosso per cortesia.

Yes, red please.

b. Ecco qui il vostro antipasto.

Here is your appetizer.

a. Buon appetito!

Enjoy your meal!

c. Anche a te!

You too!

b. Posso portare via?

Can I take everything away?

a. Si, ci potrebbe portare del pane, per favore?

Yes, could you bring us some bread, please?

b. Subito.

Immediately.

c. Il risotto era buonissimo. Ora vorrei ordinare una bistecca.

The risotto was very tasty. Now I would like to order a steak.

b. Ben cotta o al sangue?

Medium or rare?

c. Rare.

b. Vuole anche dell'insalata o delle patate arrosto?

Would you like some salad or roasted potatoes too?

c. Perché no? Un po' di insalata.

Why not, some salad.

c. Ci può portare il conto, per favore?

Can we have the check, please?

b. Ecco qui.

Here you are.

c. Posso pagare con carta di credito?

Can I pay by credit card?

b. Certamente. Ecco qui la sua ricevuta. Arrivederci.

Sure. Here is your receipt. Bye-bye.

a.c. Bye-bye!

4.7.4.1 Questions

1. A che ora aveva prenotato il tavolo Carla?

What time had Carla booked the table?

2. Che cosa ordina Carla mentre aspetta?

What does Carla order while she waits?

3. Qual è la specialità della casa?

What is the house specialty?

4. Che cosa offre il cameriere fuori menù?

What does the waiter offer off menu?

5. Che cosa prendono Mattia e Carla da bere?

What do Mattia and Carla have to drink?

6. Che cosa prendono Mattia e Carla prima del risotto?

What do Mattia and Carla have before the risotto?

7. Com'era il risotto per Mattia?

How was the risotto for Mattia?

8. Che cosa ordina Mattia dopo il risotto?

What does Mattia order after the risotto?

9. Cosa ordina di contorno Mattia?

What does Mattia order as a side dish?

10. Come paga Mattia?

How does Mattia pay?

4.7.4.2 Answer keys

1. Alle 9.

At 9 o'clock.

2. Una bottiglia di acqua frizzante.

A bottle of sparkling water.

3. Il risotto.

The risotto.

4. Risotto alla zucca con zucchine.

Pumpkin risotto with zucchini.

5. Vino rosso.

Red wine.

6. Gli antipasti.

Appetizers.

7. Molto buono.

Very tasty.

8. Una bistecca al sangue.

A rare steak.

9. Dell'insalata.

Some salad.

10. Con carta di credito.

By credit card.

Section 5 – Vocabulary

5.1 Nouns and adjectives – nomi e aggettivi

5.1.1 Nations and nationalities – nazioni e nazionalità

Italia - italiano (Italy - Italian)

Francia - francese (France - French)

Inghilterra - inglese (England - English)

Regno Unito - Britannico (United Kingdom - British)

Irlanda - irlandese (Ireland - Irish)

Germania - tedesco (Germany - German)

Spagna - spagnolo (Spain - Spanish)

Portogallo - portoghese (Portugal - Portuguese)

Stati Uniti - statunitense/americano (United States - American)

Canada - canadese (Canada - Canadian)

Cina - cinese (China - Chinese)

Giappone - giapponese (Japan - Japanese)

Russia - russo (Russia - Russian)

5.1.2 Physical appearance – aspetto fisico

Occhi piccoli/grandi/azzurri/castani/neri/verdi (small/big/blue/brown/black/green eyes)

Capelli lunghi/corti/lisci/ricci/biondi/neri/castani/rossi (long/short/straight/curly/blonde/black/brown/red hair)

Alto/basso (tall/short)

Magro/grasso (thin/fat)

5.1.3. Family – famiglia

Padre/madre (father/mother)

Nonno/nonna (grandfather/grandmother)

Genitori (parents)

Nonni (grandparents)

Parenti (relatives)

Figlio/figlia (son/daughter)

Fratello/sorella (brother/sister)

Zio/zia (uncle/aunt)

Nipote (grandson/granddaughter/nephew/niece)

5.1.4 Jobs – mestieri/lavori

Infermiere (nurse)

Avvocato (lawyer)

Traduttore (translator)

Panettiere (baker)

Macellaio (butcher)

Barista (barman)

Tassista (taxi driver)

Commesso (shop assistant)

Segretario (secretary)

Pompiere (fireman)

Imprenditore (businessman)

Operaio (factory worker)

Cameriere/cameriera (waiter/waitress)

Postino (postman)

Medico/dottore (doctor)

Cuoco (cook)

Poliziotto (policeman)

Impiegato (employee)

Giornalista (journalist)

Idraulico (plumber)

Parrucchiere (hairdresser)

Insegnante (teacher)

5.1.5 Seasons – stagioni

Autunno (fall)

Inverno (winter)

Primavera (spring)

Estate (summer)

5.1.6 Body – corpo

Viso (face)

Occhi (eyes)

Naso (nose)

Bocca (mouth)

Labbra (lips)

Testa (head)

Collo (neck)

Spalla (shoulder)

Braccio/braccia (arm/arms)
Mano (hand)
Gamba (leg)
Piede (foot)
Dito/dita (finger/fingers)

5.1.7 Medical words - parole mediche

Avere (to have got)
Mal di pancia (stomach ache)
Mal di testa (headache)
Mal di denti (toothache)
Mal di gola (sore throat)
Mal di schiena (backache)
Fare male... (to hurt)
Ex. mi fa male la gamba (my leg hurts)

5.1.8 House and furniture - casa e mobilio

Ingresso (entrance)
Salotto (living room)
Sala da pranzo (dining room)
Cucina (kitchen)
Camera da letto (bedroom)
Bagno (bathroom)
Giardino (garden)
Cantina/taverna (basement)
Balcone (balcony)
Terrazzo (terrace)
Soffitta (attic)
Scale (staircase)

Ascensore (elevator)
Pavimento (floor)
Soffitto (ceiling)
Tetto (roof)
Porta (door)
Finestra (window)
Cancello (gate)
Divano (couch)
Poltrona (armchair)
Sedia (chair)
Tavolo (table)
Letto (bed)
Lavandino (sink)
Libreria (bookshelf)
Armadio (wardrobe/closet)
Tappeto (carpet)
Tende (curtains)
Lampada (lamp)
Specchio (mirror)

5.8.1.1 Objects and tools – oggetti e strumenti

[kitchen]
Forchetta (fork)
Coltello (knife)
Cucchiaio (spoon)
Cucchiaino (teaspoon)
Bicchiere (glass)
Tazza (cup)

Tazzina (small cup)
Tovaglia (tablecloth)
Tovagliolo (napkin)
Piatto piano (plate)
Piatto fondo (soup plate)
Fornelli (stove)
Forno (oven)
Frigorifero (fridge)
Congelatore (freezer)
Lavandino (sink)

[bathroom]
Asciugamano (towel)
Accappatoio (bathrobe)
Spazzolino (toothbrush)
Dentifricio (toothpaste)
Spazzola (hairbrush)
Pettine (comb)
Rasoio (razor)
Bagnoschiuma (bath gel)
Docciaschiuma (shower gel)
Asciugacapelli (hair dryer)
Doccia (shower)
Vasca da bagno (bathtub)

[bedroom]
Lenzuolo (sheet)
Coperta (blanket)
Cuscino (pillow)

Pigiama (pyjamas)

5.1.9 In the street – in strada

Strisce pedonali (crosswalk)

Incrocio (intersection)

Semaforo (traffic light)

Ponte (bridge)

Zona pedonale (pedestrian area)

Via (street)

Viale (avenue)

Piazza (square)

Rotonda (rotary)

Corsia dei taxi o degli autobus (taxi or bus lane)

Autostrada (highway)

Fermata dell'autobus, della metro, del tram (tram, subway, and bus stop)

A destra/sinistra (on the right/left)

5.1.10 In the city – in città

Chiesa (church)

Ufficio postale (postal office)

Scuola (school)

Comune (town hall)

Supermercato (supermarket)

Mercato (market)

Ristorante (restaurant)

Albergo (hotel)

Parco giochi (playground)

Libreria (bookshop)

Farmacia (drugstore)

Fruttivendolo (fruit seller)

Gioielleria (jewelry shop)

Macelleria (butcher shop)

Panificio (bakery)

Fioraio (flower shop)

5.1.11 Clothes and accessories – abbigliamento e accessori

Maglione (sweater)

Orecchini (earrings)

Occhiali da vista/da sole (eye/sunglasses)

Scarpe (shoes)

Calze (socks)

Collana (necklace)

Camicia (shirt)

Gonna (skirt)

Sciarpa (scarf)

Anello (ring)

Stivali (boots)

Guanti (gloves)

Cintura (belt)

Bracciale (bracelet)

Pantaloni (trousers)

Cappotto (coat)

Cappello (hat)

Tuta (track suit)

Costume da bagno (swim suit)

Vestito/abito da donna/uomo (dress/suit)

Maglietta (T-shirt)

Giacca (jacket)

5.1.12 The Weather – il meteo/tempo

Che tempo fa? (what's the weather like?)

Piove (it rains)

Nevica (it snows)

C'è il sole/è soleggiato (it is sunny)

C'è vento/è ventilato (it is windy)

Ci sono le nuvole/è nuvoloso (it is cloudy)

C'è nebbia (it is foggy)

Fa caldo (it is hot)

Fa freddo (it is cold)

C'è umidità/è umido (it is wet)

La pioggia (the rain)

La neve (the snow)

Il sole (the sun)

La nebbia (the fog)

Il vento (the wind)

5.1.13 Feelings and emotions – sentimenti ed emozioni

arrabbiato (angry)

rabbia (anger)

contento/felice (happy)

felicità (happiness)

deluso (disappointed)

delusione (disappointment)

imbarazzato (embarrassed)

imbarazzo (embarrassment)

orgoglioso (proud)
orgoglio (pride)
triste (sad)
tristezza (sadness)
timido (shy)
timidezza (shyness)

5.1.14 The environment – l'ambiente

Mare (sea)
Spiaggia (beach)
Costa (coast/shore)
Montagna (mountain)
Collina (hill)
Fiume (river)
Lago (lake)
Cascata (waterfall)
Deserto (desert)
Foresta (forest)
Giungla (jungle)

5.1.15 Means of transport – mezzi di trasporto

Macchina/automobile (car)
Motorino (motor-scooter)
Moto (motorbike)
Bicicletta/bici (bicycle/bike)
Barca (boat)
Nave (ship)
Traghetto (ferry)
Camion (truck)

Tir (lorry)

Aereo (airplane)

Elicottero (helicopter)

5.1.16 Animals - animali

5.1.16.1 In the farm - nella fattoria

Mucca (cow)

Toro (bull)

Maiale (pig)

Pecora (ship)

Cavallo (horse)

Asino (donkey)

Gallina (hen)

Gallo (rooster)

Coniglio (rabbit)

5.1.16.2. Pets - animali domestici

Cane (dog)

Gatto (cat)

Pesce rosso (goldfish)

Criceto (hamster)

5.1.16.3 Wild animals - animali selvatici

Scimmia (monkey)

Squalo (shark)

Lupo (wolf)

Giraffa (giraffe)

Cammello (camel)

Gufo (owl)

Tigre (tiger)

Orso (bear)

Balena (whale)

Leone (lion)

Coccodrillo (crocodile)

Delfino (dolphin)

Elefante (elephant)

Scoiattolo (squirrel)

Serpente (snake)

Canguro (kangaroo)

Volpe (fox)

Pipistrello (bat)

Rana (frog)

Topo (mouse)

5.1.17. Food – cibo

5.1.17.1 Vegetables – verdure

Carciofo (artichoke)

Spinaci (spinach)

Piselli (peas)

Aglio (garlic)

Cipolla (onion)

Zucca (pumpkin)

Funghi (mushrooms)

Sedano (celery)

Melanzana (eggplant)

Carota (carrot)

Patata (potato)

Pomodoro (tomato)

Fagioli (beans)

Fagiolini (green beans)

Peperone (pepper)

Zucchina (zucchini)

Lattuga (lettuce)

5.1.17.2. Fruits – frutta

Fico (fig)

Pesca (peach)

Ananas (pineapple)

Oliva (olive)

Banana (banana)

Anguria (watermelon)

Mela (apple)

Castagne (chestnuts)

Fragola (strawberry)

Grappolo d'uva (grapes)

Cocco (coconut)

Noccioline (peanuts)

Noce (walnut)

Mais (corn)

Limone (lemon)

Arancia (orange)

Ciliegia (cherry)

Albicocca (apricot)

5.1.17.3. Meat – carne

Pollo (chicken)

Manzo (beef)

Agnello (lamb)

Maiale (pork)

Tacchino (turkey)

Anatra (duck)

Bistecca (steak)

Salsiccia (sausage)

Prosciutto (ham)

Pancetta (bacon)

5.1.17.4 Fish and seafood – pesce e frutti di mare

Meluzzo (cod)

Salmone (salmon)

Tonno (tuna)

Polpo (octopus)

Gambero (shrimp)

Cozze (mussels)

Ostrica (oyster)

Aragosta (lobster)

Granchio (crab)

Sardina/acciuga (sardine)

5.1.17.5. Dairy foods – latticini

Formaggio (cheese)

Burro (butter)

Panna (cream)

Latte (milk)

Parmigiano (parmesan cheese)

5.1.17.6. Others – altri

Pane (bread)

Maionese (mayonnaise)

Olio (oil)

Sale (salt)

Pepe (pepper)

Gelato (ice cream)

Uovo/uova (egg/eggs)

Patatine fritte (French fries)

Patate al forno (baked potatoes)

Pasta (pasta)

Zuppa (soup)

Riso (rice)

Polpette (meatballs)

Ciambella (donut)

Biscotti (cookies)

Torta (pie)

5.1.18. Colors - colori

Arancione (orange)

Argento (silver)

Azzurro (light blue)

Bianco (white)

Blu (blue)

Dorato (golden)

Giallo (yellow)

Grigio (gray)

Marrone (brown)

Nero (black)

Rosa (pink)

Rosso (red)

Verde (green)

Viola (purple)

Chiaro (light)

Scuro (dark)

Pallido (pale)

5.1.19. Sports – sport

Atletica (athletics)

Calcio (soccer)

Canotaggio (rowing)

Ciclismo (cycling)

Equitazione (horse riding)

Ginnastica (gym)

Nuoto (swimming)

Pallacanestro (basketball)

Pallavolo (volleyball)

Pugilato (boxing)

Sci (ski)

5.1.20 Italian holidays – festività italiane

1 novembre, Ognissanti – November 1st, All Saints' Day

(in the past, this was a Catholic feast, but nowadays, it's only a day to relax after Halloween night and to realize that winter is coming)

8 dicembre, Immacolata Concezione – December 8th, Immaculate Conception

(historically, it represents the day when Mary became pregnant through the holy spirit; now it is a day dedicated to Christmas decorations and marks the countdown to Christmas holidays)

25 dicembre, Giorno di Natale – December 25th, Christmas Day

26 dicembre, Santo Stefano - December 26th, the day after Christmas

1 gennaio, Capodanno - January 1st, New Year's Day

6 gennaio, Epifania - January 1st, Epiphany

(it is a small version of Christmas; an ugly old woman puts sweeties and candies inside socks. It marks the end of Christmas holidays)

Pasqua - Easter Sunday

Pasquetta - Easter Monday

25 aprile, Festa della Liberazione - April 25th, Liberation Day

(this day commerates the end of Nazi occupation of the country during World War II and the victory of the resistance)

1 maggio, Festa del Lavoro - May 1st, Labor Day

2 giugno, Festa della Repubblica - June 2nd, Republic Day

(when Italy signed the democratic republic system after a Fascist government)

15 agosto, Ferragosto - August 15th

(before it was a Catholic feast, but now represents the highest peak of summer holidays; at night, people watch the sky to see falling stars)

5.1.21 Parts of the car - parti della macchina

Sportello/portiera (door)

Volante (steering wheel)

Cintura di sicurezza (safety belt)

Cruscotto (dashboard)

Contachilometri (odometer)

Leva del cambio (gear level)

Cambio automatico (automatic transmission)

Freno (brake)

Acceleratore (throttle)

Pneumatico/ruota (tyre)

Serbatoio benzina/carburante (fuel tank)

Specchietto retrovisore (rearview mirror)

Specchietto laterale (side-view mirror)

Fanale anteriore/posteriore (headlight/tailight)

Sedile (car seat)

Indicatore direzione/freccia (turn signal)

Parabrezza (windshield)

Tergicristallo (wiper)

5.2 Most commons verbs – verbi più comuni

Accendere (to switch on)

[past participle "acceso"]

Accettare (to accept)

Aggiustare (to fix)

Aiutare (to help)

Alzarsi (to wake up)

Amare (to love)

Aprire (to open)

[past participle "aperto"]

Andare (to go)

[presente indicative "io vado, tu vai, egli/ella va, noi andiamo, voi andate, loro vanno]

Arrivare (to arrive)

Ascoltare (to listen)

Aspettare (to wait)

Attraversare (to cross)

Aver bisogno di (to need)

Avere caldo (to be hot)

Avere fame (to be hungry)

Avere freddo (to be cold)

Avere paura (to be scared)

Avere ragione (to be right)

Avere sete (to be thirsty)

Avere sonno (to be tired)

Avere torto (to be wrong)

Ballare (to dance)

Bere (to drink)

[presente indicative "io bevo, tu bevi, egli/ella beve, noi beviamo, voi bevete, loro bevono]

Bollire (to boil)

Cadere (to fall)

Cambiare (to change)

Camminare (to walk)

Cancellare (to cancel)

Cantare (to sing)

Capire (to understand)

[presente indicative "io capisco, tu capisci, egli/ella capisce, noi capiamo, voi capite, loro capiscono]

Cenare (to have dinner)

Chiamare (to call)

Chiedere (to ask)

[past participle "chiesto"]

Chiudere (to close)

[past participle "chiuso"]

Cominciare (to begin)

Comprare (to buy)

Contare (to count)

Correre (to run)

[past participle "corso"]

Costare (to cost)

Costruire (to build)

[presente indicative "io costruisco, tu costruisci, egli/ella costruisce, noi costruiamo, voi costruite, loro costruiscono]

Credere (to believe)

Crescere (to grow)

[presente indicative "io cresco, tu cresci, egli/ella cresce, noi cresciamo, voi crescete, loro crescono]

[past participle "cresciuto"]

Cuocere (to cook)

[presente indicative "io cuocio, tu cuoci, egli/ella cuoce, noi cuociamo, voi cuocete, loro cuociono]

[past participle "cotto"]

Dare (to give)

[presente indicative "io do, tu dai, egli/ella dà, noi diamo, voi date, loro danno]

Dare una festa (to have a party)

Decidere (to decide)

[past participle "deciso"]

Dimenticare (to forget)

Dire (to say/to tell)

[presente indicative "io dico, tu dici, egli/ella dice, noi diciamo, voi dite, loro dicono]

[past participle "detto"]

Diventare (to become)

Divertirsi (to have fun)

Dormire (to sleep)

Entrare (to get in)

Fare (to do/to make)

[presente indicative "io faccio, tu fai, egli/ella fa, noi facciamo, voi fate, loro fanno]

[past participle "fatto"]

Fare colazione (to have breakfast)

Farsi la barba (to shave)

Farsi la doccia/il bagno (to have a shower/a bath)

Fare un riposino (to have a nap)

Fermarsi (to stop)

Finire (to finish/to end)

[presente indicative "io finisco, tu finisci, egli/ella finisce, noi finiamo, voi finite, loro finiscono]

Fumare (to smoke)

Giocare (to play)

Girare (to turn)

Guardare (to look)

Guidare (to drive)

Imparare (to learn)

Incontrare/conoscere (to meet)

[presente indicative "io conosco, tu conisci, egli/ella conosce, noi conosciamo, voi conoscete, loro conscono]

[past participle "conosciuto"]

Indossare (to wear)

Insegnare (to teach)

Iscriversi (to sign up/to register/to enroll)

Lasciare (to let/to leave)

Lavare (to wash)

Lavorare (to work)

Leggere (to read)

[past participle "letto"]

Mangiare (to eat)

Mandare (to send)

Mescolare (to stir)

Morire (to die)

[presente indicative "io muoio, tu muori, egli/ella muore, noi moriamo, voi morite, loro muoiono]

[past participle "morto"]

Nascere (to be born)

[presente indicative "io nasco, tu nasci, egli/ella nasce, noi nasciamo, voi nascete, loro nascono]

[past participle "nato"]

Nuotare (to swim)

Offrire (to offer)

[presente indicative "io offro, tu offri, egli/ella offre, noi offriamo, voi offrite, loro offrono]

[past participle "offerto"]

Ordinare (to order)

Pagare (to pay)

Parlare (to speak)

Partire (to leave)

Passare (to pass by)

Pensare (to think)

Perdere/Mancare (to lose/to miss)

[past participle "perso"]

Pettinare (to comb)

Portare (to bring)

Pranzare (to have lunch)

Prendere (to take)

[past participle "preso"]

Preoccuparsi (to worry)

Preparare (to prepare)

Pulire (to clean)

[presente indicative "io pulisco, tu pulisci, egli/ella pulisce, noi puliamo, voi pulite, loro puliscono]

Restare (to stay)

[past participle "rimasto"]

Ricevere (to receive)

Ricordare (to remember)

Ridere (to laugh)

[past participle "riso"]

Riempire (to fill)

Rispondere (to answer/to reply)

[past participle "risposto"]

Ritornare (to come back)

Rompere (to brake)

[past participle "rotto"]

Rubare (to steal)

Salire (to come up)

[presente indicative "io salgo, tu sali, egli/ella sale, noi saliamo, voi salite, loro salgono]

Scegliere (to choose)

[presente indicative "io scelgo, tu scegli, egli/ella sceglie, noi scegliamo, voi scegliete, loro scelgono]

[past participle "scelto"]

Scendere (to climb down/to get off)

[past participle "sceso"]

Scrivere (to write)

[past participle "scritto"]

Sembrare (to look like/ to seem like)

Sentire/provare (to feel)

Sentire (to hear)

Significare (to mean)

Sollevare (to lift)

Sparire (to disappear)

[presente indicative "io sparisco, tu sparisci, egli/ella sparisce, noi spariamo, voi sparite, loro spariscono]

Spegnere (to switch off)

[presente indicative "io spengo, tu spegni, egli/ella spegne, noi spegniamo, voi spegnete, loro spengono]

[past participle "spento"]

Spendere/trascorrere (to spend)

[past participle "speso/trascorso"]

Spiegare (to exaplain)

Spostare (to move)

Studiare (to study)

Suonare (to ring/to play)

Tagliare (to cut)

Telefonare (to phone)

Tenere (to hold/to keep)

[presente indicative "io tengo, tu tieni, egli/ella tiene, noi teniamo, voi tenete, loro tengono]

Tradurre (to translate)

[past participle "tradotto"]

Traslocare (to move – "to change place")

Trovare (to find)

Truccarsi (to put on makeup)

Usare (to use)

Uscire (to go out)

[presente indicative "io esco, tu esci, egli/ella esce, noi usciamo, voi uscite, loro escono]

Vedere (to see/to watch)

[past participle "visto"]

Vendere (to sell)

Venire (to come)

[presente indicative "io vengo, tu vieni, egli/ella viene, noi veniamo, voi venite, loro vengono]

Vestirsi (to get dressed)

Viaggiare (to travel)

Vincere (to win)

[past participle "vinto"]

Vivere (to live)

[past participle "vissuto"]

Volare (to fly)

Conclusion

Whatever your reason for learning Italian, this book should have been useful and provided you with the basic tools to be able to explain yourself and understand an elementary conversation.

The first two sections explained basic grammar rules, comparing them with the English language, which should have given you both an aid to learning them easily shown you how important the grammar is. In fact, even if it could be considered something "technical" by many, something reserved for "experts", it actually gives you tools to manage words and phrases so that you can communicate efficiently in any situation.

The third section gave you the chance to test yourself by putting into practice what you learned in sections 1 and 2 and to go back to those sections if there was something you didn't get right.

As stated in the introduction, the main aim of a language is communication. And what is very important and essential is to understand and to be understood everywhere by everyone. Section 4 showed you how Italian grammar rules are used in real and common situations, "how they work" in practice. As suggested, you should have tried to replicate dialogues pretending to be one of the characters involved, and this is something you should carry on doing to improve your language level, and also by changing the sentences and words.

Language is still an ordered mix of words that translate what is in your mind, what you are thinking, and what you want to say. Thus, the function of the last section was to give you essential words and basic expressions so you can express yourself on any occasion.

Of course, the path is long. There are still many aspects, grammar rules, tenses, words, and expressions of the Italian language that you didn't learn in this book, but these four sections have certainly given you the basic tools, which represent a good starting point!

Remember, learning a language is an endless journey. During it, you will encounter difficulties, but don't be discouraged! In the end, you will be rewarded with the most exciting prize: the knowledge of a new language. And this means the opportunity to communicate and express yourself to and with other people, and to get into a new culture, having the possibility to understand it from an inner point of view.

Check out another book by Language Equipped Travelers

www.ingramcontent.com/pod-product-compliance
Lightning Source LLC
Chambersburg PA
CBHW070047230426
43661CB00005B/794